LIGHTHOUSES OF MASSACHUSETTS

Help Us Keep This Guide Up to Date

Every effort has been made by the authors and editors to make this guide as accurate and useful as possible. However, many things can change after a guide is published—phone numbers change, facilities come under new management, etc.

We would love to hear from you concerning your experiences with this guide and how you feel it could be improved and be kept up to date. While we may not be able to respond to all comments and suggestions, we'll take them to heart and we'll also make certain to share them with the authors. Please send your comments and suggestions to the following address:

The Globe Pequot Press
Reader Response/Editorial Department
P. O. Box 480
Guilford, CT 06437

Or you may e-mail us at:

editorial@GlobePequot.com

Thanks for your input, and happy travels!

LIGHTHOUSES OF MASSACHUSETTS

A Guidebook and Keepsake

Bruce Roberts and Ray Jones

INSIDERS' GUIDE®

GUILFORD, CONNECTICUT

AN IMPRINT OF THE GLOBE PEQUOT PRESS

387.1
ROB

INSIDERS' GUIDE®

Text design by Schwartzman Design, Deep River, CT
Map design and terrain by Stephen C. Stringall, Cartography by M.A. Dubé
Map © The Globe Pequot Press
All photographs are by Bruce Roberts unless otherwise noted.

Library of Congress Cataloging-in-Publication Data
Robert, Bruce, 1930-
    Lighthouses of Massachusetts : a guidebook and keepsake / Bruce Roberts and Ray
Jones.—1st ed
        p. cm. — (Lighthouses series)
    ISBN 0-7627-3737-9
        1. Lighthouses—Massachusetts—History 2. Lighthouses—Massachusetts—Guidebooks.
I. Jones, Ray, 1948- II. Title. III. Lighthouses series (Globe Pequot Press)

    VK1024.M35R63 2005
    387.1'55'09744—dc22

                                                                    2004060868

Manufactured in China
First Edition/First Printing

NOV 1 9 2007
Cent

The information listed in this guide was confirmed at press time. The ownership of many
lighthouses, however, is gradually being transferred from the Coast Guard to private
concerns. Please confirm visitor information before traveling.

DEDICATION

For John Fitzgerald Kennedy, a man of the sea

ACKNOWLEDGMENTS

We would like to thank Shirin Pagels, president of the New England Lighthouse Lovers, for her many wonderful photographs that we included in this book. Shirin's love of lighthouses shows through.

CONTENTS

Oil stored in this small brick building once fueled the lamps of the Marblehead Lighthouse, which marked the entrance to Salem Harbor. The station's cast-iron tower, a rarity in New England, soars in the distance.

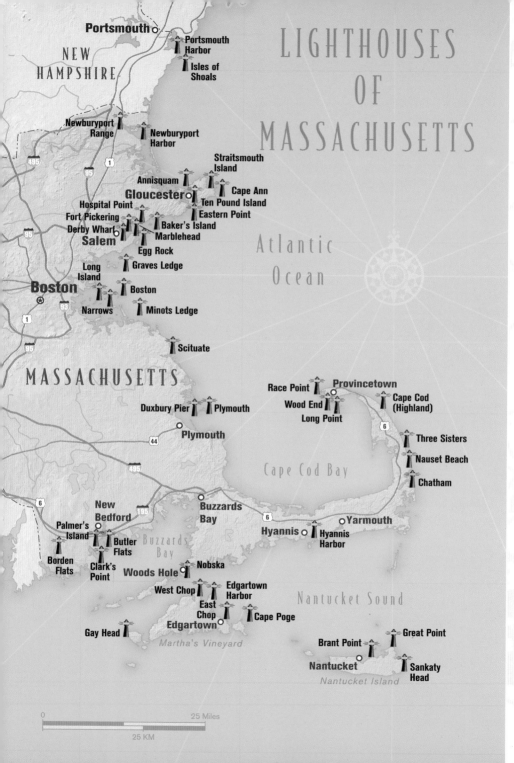

LIGHTHOUSES
OF
MASSACHUSETTS

NEW HAMPSHIRE

Portsmouth

Portsmouth Harbor

Isles of Shoals

Newburyport Range

Newburyport Harbor

Straitsmouth Island

Annisquam

Cape Ann

Gloucester

Ten Pound Island

Hospital Point

Eastern Point

Fort Pickering

Baker's Island

Derby Wharf

Marblehead

Salem

Egg Rock

Long Island

Graves Ledge

Boston

Boston

Narrows

Minots Ledge

Scituate

MASSACHUSETTS

Atlantic Ocean

Race Point

Provincetown

Wood End

Cape Cod (Highland)

Long Point

Duxbury Pier

Plymouth

Plymouth

Three Sisters

Nauset Beach

Chatham

Cape Cod Bay

New Bedford

Buzzards Bay

Palmer's Island

Hyannis

Hyannis Harbor

Yarmouth

Butler Flats

Buzzards Bay

Borden Flats

Clark's Point

Nobska

Woods Hole

West Chop

Edgartown Harbor

East Chop

Cape Poge

Gay Head

Edgartown

Nantucket Sound

Martha's Vineyard

Brant Point

Great Point

Nantucket

Sankaty Head

Nantucket Island

0   25 Miles

25 KM

INTRODUCTION

Massachusetts is the cradle not only of American independence but also of the national system of maritime lights that has allowed the country to grow and prosper. As a British colony, Massachusetts gave rise not just to the Boston Tea Party and the "Shot Heard Round the World" but also to the first lighthouse in North America. In fact several Massachusetts lighthouses are among the oldest in the United States, and all have played important roles in our nation's history.

As its nickname suggests, the Bay State has always been married to the sea, and it was maritime lights that helped make that bond permanent. The Pilgrims took refuge here after a stormy Atlantic crossing—perhaps guided to sheltered waters off Plymouth by the light of campfires set by Native American fishermen. The Pilgrims' *Mayflower* reached America safely, but many other vessels would not be so fortunate. With no beacons to mark navigable channels and deadly hazards, they ended up as piles of shattered timber on the beaches of Cape Cod or the jagged rocks that line the shore of Massachusetts Bay.

The coast of early colonial Massachusetts was a dark and deadly place, and only the bravest or most foolhardy sea captains brought their vessels here. Some were adventurous enough to try, however, and they helped maintain a tenuous link between the colony and Europe. In time more and more ships found their way to Plymouth, Salem, and Boston, and importers grew wealthy on profits from the overseas trade. By the early eighteenth century, merchants were demanding that colonial officials take steps to make it easier and safer for ships to reach port. The only practical way to do this was to build lighthouses.

Boston Lights the Way

The first true lighthouse in North America stood on a small, nearly-barren island a few miles east of Boston. Time and again, Boston-bound ships had wrecked while searching in vain for the harbor entrance, dumping their cargoes, passengers, and crews into the churning surf. Weary of the human and financial losses suffered in these calamities, businessmen in Boston petitioned the colonial government for funds to establish a "Light House and Lanthorn on Some Head Land for the Direction of Ships and Vessels in the Night

Time." The result was the Boston Lighthouse, a rough masonry tower on what was then called Beacon Island—today it is known as Little Brewster Island. The enclosed lantern at the top was equipped with simple tallow candles that were lit at dusk and required the close attention of a keeper throughout the night. A simple, though adequate, two-story house was provided for the keeper and his family.

The lighthouse was completed during early autumn 1716, and on September 14 keeper George Worthylake, a local harbor pilot and shepherd, climbed to the top of the new stone tower. There, with the sun descending in the west and a blanket of darkness racing across the ocean from the east, Worthylake put a match to the station's candles for the very first time. On that night and the many thousands of nights since, the masters of ships headed for Boston have seen a light at the edge of the harbor and known that safe waters lay ahead. Although its beacon is no longer produced by candles, mariners still see the Boston Lighthouse today, almost three centuries after it first shined out over the harbor.

A Lighthouse Tragedy

Attracted like schools of fish by the light on Beacon Island, ships crowded the docks in Boston, and merchants there prospered. Unfortunately, the lighthouse proved far less profitable for Worthylake. His meager salary of fifty pounds a year was supposed to have been supplemented by the fees he earned as a harbor pilot, but his arduous responsibilities as keeper left little time for any other work.

To help feed and clothe his family, Worthylake ran herds of sheep on nearby islands, but the keeper had no more luck as a shepherd than he did as a pilot. During a terrible winter gale in 1717, several dozen of his sheep wandered onto a spit where they were soon stranded by the tide. Since he could not abandon his post in a storm, Worthylake was forced to watch in despair as the hapless animals washed off the spit and into the sea. The loss of his sheep all but bankrupted the keeper; to help ease his financial difficulties, colonial officials agreed to increase his salary to seventy pounds.

The extra money was welcome, but Worthylake never got to spend it. He and several members of his family drowned when their small boat capsized only a 100 yards or so from the safety of the lighthouse dock. Ironically, the bodies washed ashore on the same spit where the Worthylake sheep had perished only a few months earlier. And the money Worthylake had received in Boston had mysteriously vanished.

By the time of the Revolutionary War, lighthouses had been built at a number of key locations along the Massachusetts coast and throughout the colonies. In 1746 the island of Nantucket had established a maritime beacon at Brant Point to guide its whaling fleet into harbor. In 1769 the historic community of Plymouth had built a lighthouse on the Gurnet, a long, fish-shaped peninsula at the entrance to Plymouth Bay. In 1771 an impressive twin-towered light had been established on Thatcher Island off Cape Ann northeast of Boston, and that same year New Hampshire colonial officials had set up a light at Fort William and Mary to point the way to Portsmouth. Other colonies had also followed Boston's example and built light-houses. Among them were the Beavertail Lighthouse (1749) near the entrance to Rhode Island's Narragansett Bay; the New London Harbor Lighthouse (1760) in Connecticut; the Sandy Hook Light-house (1764) in New Jersey; the Cape Henlopen Lighthouse (1765) in Delaware; and the Charleston Lighthouse in South Carolina (1767). These colonial beacons had attracted a trickle, then a river, and finally a flood of maritime commerce, and although it might not have seemed so at the time, they had lit the fires of revolt.

"Two If By Sea"

On the night of April 18, 1775, Paul Revere watched for a signal from a makeshift lighthouse—the steeple of Boston's Old North Church. Soon a fellow patriot would raise a lantern in the steeple and send Revere riding hell-bent for Concord and Lexington and shouting his famous message: "The British are coming!" No doubt, while he waited, Revere occasionally took his eyes off the steeple to glance eastward toward the menacing British fleet hovering just outside Boston Harbor. Looking in that direction, the silversmith's sharp eyes might have caught the faint glimmer of the maritime light on Beacon (Little Brewster) Island. That light would prove at least as important to the cause of American independence as the one Revere would shortly see in the Old North Church steeple.

Built almost sixty years earlier, the harbor lighthouse had guided countless thousands of trading ships to Boston's wharves and, in

This little lighthouse is a favorite of summertime tourists and ferry passengers approaching the old whaling port of Nantucket. The Brant Point beacon has guided mariners into Nantucket Harbor since 1746.

this way, contributed mightily to the prosperity of the colonies. That same prosperity had convinced the British that their upstart colonists should pay for the protection of King George's fleet and other expensive services rendered by the mother country. So Parliament decided to tax the colonies. American businessmen, who to this day don't smile at the thought of taxes, responded hostilely, even to Parliament's penny-a-pound tax on tea. In Boston a party of anti-tax demonstrators painted their faces, dressed up like Indians, and ceremoniously dumped a shipload of Chinese tea into the harbor. The British retaliated by blockading Boston with their fleet. Massachusetts city dwellers and farmers started hoarding gunpowder and calling themselves Minutemen. People began to talk openly about independence from England and, having seen a light in a church steeple, Revere found himself riding through the night toward Lexington.

Meanwhile, the British had taken over the lighthouse and were operating it themselves as a beacon for their warships. To strike back at the blockading fleet, the Minutemen decided to put out the light. Early in July 1775 a small detachment of American troops landed near the light station and set fire to the lighthouse. To observers on the mainland, the burning tower seemed a great torch "ascending up to Heaven." The flames confused gunners on the British warships, who tried but failed to blast the Minutemen out of the water as they retreated back to Boston.

The raid appeared to have been a complete success, but the lighthouse had not been totally destroyed. No sooner had the scorched tower cooled than the British put laborers ashore on Beacon Island to begin repairs. A contingent of royal marines stood guard while the carpenters sawed lumber and pounded nails.

News of the rapidly progressing repair work soon reached Boston, where General George Washington had recently taken over command of the Continental Army. Washington felt he could not allow the tower to be relit and decided to send a second raiding party to the island. On July 30 some 300 Continental soldiers led by Major Benjamin Tupper set out for Beacon Island in whaleboats. Aided by darkness, the Americans caught the redcoat marines by surprise and quickly defeated them. Hurriedly undoing the work of the British carpenters, the raiders set fire to everything that would burn and escaped thanks to the timely assistance of an artillery piece on nearby Nantasket Head. The Americans lost only one soldier in the fight, while their opponents suffered heavy casualties. Washington called the action "gallant and soldier-like" and praised his soldiers for so adroitly "possessing themselves of the enemie's [*sic*] post at the lighthouse."

A Patriot Falls

Although the harbor was now dark and unsafe for nighttime navigation, the blockade continued. Several of the king's frigates remained near the harbor entrance, harassing fishermen and threatening coastal towns and villages. The continued presence of enemy vessels

Established in 1716, Boston Lighthouse is America's oldest navigational station. British troops destroyed the original tower during the Revolutionary War, and the existing structure replaced it in 1783.

enraged Samuel Adams, the Boston firebrand who had more or less invented the American Revolution. Unable to stomach the sight of the British ships, Adams devised a plan to force them out of the harbor. The effectiveness of the gun at Nantasket Head during Tupper's raid on the lighthouse may have helped hatch the scheme. The Americans would land troops on Nantasket Head and various strategic islands in the harbor, fortify them, and drive the blockaders away with artillery. On June 13, 1776, only three weeks before the former colonies officially declared their independence from Britain,

armed boats once more set sail from Boston and headed for the outer harbor. By dawn on the following day, Continental Army gunners had their cannon ready, and the pounding began.

The British awoke to a fiery rain of shot and shell, and soon they were raising sails and racing for the open sea. Before weighing anchor, however, they sent a raiding party of their own to Beacon Island. They were determined that if the Royal Navy could not have the lighthouse, neither could the Americans. British sailors hurriedly stacked gunpowder inside the lighthouse tower, lit a slow-burning fuse, and ran for their boats. When the fuse had burned down to its end, it ignited a blast so powerful that it could be heard several miles away in Boston. The explosion split apart the old stone tower, and what remained of it collapsed into the ocean. When Massachusetts officials again visited Beacon Island, they found to their dismay that America's tallest patriot, the Boston Lighthouse, had fallen.

Three Centuries of Service

The Boston Lighthouse lay in ruins until the Revolutionary War was over. In 1783 the Massachusetts legislature raised 1,450 pounds sterling to restore the lighthouse, and by the end of that year, it was back in operation. Its lantern has never been dark since. In 2016 the station will begin its fourth century of service to mariners.

A sheet of paper attached to the wall of the Boston Lighthouse helps put its extraordinary history in perspective. It lists the names of more than sixty keepers who have served there. The first name on the list is that of the unfortunate George Worthylake. The second is Robert Saunders who, ironically, suffered the same fate as his predecessor: He drowned in a boating accident after only a few weeks on the job.

Undaunted by the misfortunes of the station's earlier keepers, Captain John Hayes replaced Saunders and not only survived but managed to prosper during his fifteen-year stay on the island. So, too, did most of the other keepers who lived on this rocky island and tended Boston Lighthouse. Some remained on the job much longer than Hayes. Robert Ball kept the light from 1733 until shortly before the Revolution, a stretch of more than forty years. Tom Bates held the post of Boston Lighthouse keeper from the end of the Civil War to the 1890s.

The station's last civilian keeper was Maurice Babcock, who served from 1926 until the beginning of World War II, by which time the 150-year-old U.S. Lighthouse Service (1789–1939) had been absorbed by the Coast Guard. Babcock's replacement was Ralph Norwood, a coastguardsman who kept the light throughout the war years and left the island in 1945.

Among the last to add his name to the list of keepers was Dennis Devers, a young coastguardsman posted to the Boston Light during the 1980s. "It's a life apart," Devers has said. "But it also makes you feel a part of something meaningful—history, nature, whatever you want to call it."

A keeper at any lighthouse in any era might have said the same—but no longer. The profession of lighthouse keeper is extinct, at least in this country. Over the years the Coast Guard has increased efficiency and cut costs by automating lighthouses and removing their keepers. By the 1990s the historic Boston Lighthouse was the last maritime light in America with an official resident keeper. Then, in 1998, the Boston Light itself was finally automated. Some say this brought the age of lighthouses to a close, but read this book and visit a few historic Massachusetts light stations and you'll find ample reason to disagree. Although sophisticated electronics now make it possible to pinpoint a ship's position, the masters of vessels great and small do occasionally look to lighthouses for guidance. And for the rest of us, they perform an even more important function: Lighthouses serve as reminders that life is an adventure, that sometimes we need a light to lead us out of the darkness, and that we are connected to something meaningful—history, nature, whatever you want to call it.

Former lighthouse keeper Dennis Devers polishes Boston Light's big Fresnel lens. Most such classic lenses have been replaced by modern optics that are easier to maintain.

How to Use This Guide

It is still possible to experience the feeling described by keeper Dennis Devers. Read about the beautiful and historic towers featured in this book. Then, if you like, visit them and see for yourself.

The Bay State boasts more than thirty standing lighthouses, and every one is worth a look. This book takes you to most every Massachusetts lighthouse that can be reached, as well as some that are inaccessible, and one New Hampshire lighthouse along the state border. It also takes a loving backward glance at a few "lost lights," Massachusetts lighthouses that were once vital to mariners but vanished long ago.

The book is divided into four sections: Portsmouth to Salem; Boston to Plymouth; Provincetown to Fall River; and Nantucket and Martha's Vineyard. Within the sections lighthouses are presented geographically. This arrangement should make it easier to plan your own Massachusetts lighthouse outings—so should the directions, telephone contacts, and other travel information included at the end of each listing.

Under normal circumstances you should be able to visit the most attractive and historic lighthouses in one or another of the sections mentioned above in a single long-weekend excursion from Boston. To help you select the lighthouses you want to visit, individual listings include advice in the form of simple symbols: 🏛 for lighthouses that are especially historic—most of them are; 🚪 for lighthouses that are accessible—by car, boat or foot; 🗣 for visitor-friendly lighthouses that are frequently open to the public and feature museums or similar attractions; 📷 for lighthouse that make great pictures—most of them are quite photogenic; and 🎬 for "Lost Lighthouses," historic towers that, unfortunately, no longer exist. For added convenience each listing also includes an easy-to-read summary of key information on the lighthouse: location; date the light was established (date the light first shined); tower height; elevation of the focal plane; type of optic; current status; characteristic; range; and, for all active lighthouses, the precise latitude and longitude of the station.

We hope you enjoy your Massachusetts lighthouse adventure.

CHAPTER ONE:
PORTSMOUTH, NEW HAMPSHIRE TO SALEM, MASSACHUSETTS

A wash in history and bright with maritime beacons, the coastline north of Boston is a good place to test the strong bonds that link lighthouses to America's past and future. Likely, the best place to start is the colonial city of Portsmouth, N.H., home of one of the oldest navigational lights in the United States.

From Boston you can reach Portsmouth by interstate in little more than an hour, but in 1775 it would have taken a hard-riding courier more than a day to make the same journey. In June of that year, a weary messenger arrived in Portsmouth with news that British forces were gathering in Boston for an assault on patriot positions outside the city. Sympathetic New Hampshire militiamen responded by marching south alongside wagonloads of gunpowder and other martial supplies—the spoils of a raid on a British supply depot near the Portsmouth Harbor Lighthouse. Later, that same gunpowder would be fired into the faces of redcoats advancing on Bunker Hill and would help prove the metal of Continental forces.

The Portsmouth Harbor Light still shines today, more than 225 years after the revolution. Your best view of the light may be from the water—year-round harbor cruises are available.

Another colonial lighthouse guards Cape Ann and the northern approaches to Massachusetts Bay. The station is famous for its twin towers, although only one remains in use today. Both were still shining in 1919 when the Cape Ann Lights warned the passenger liner *America* away from rocks and helped save the life of President Woodrow Wilson. If not for this, Wilson's trip to the Versailles peace conference might have ended tragically.

About halfway between Cape Ann and Boston is the once-thriving port of Salem. If not for its notorious seventeenth-century witch trials, Salem might be known today as the "City of Lighthouses." At least half a dozen key navigational lights still point the way to Salem Harbor. Perhaps the most historic and charming of them is the little Derby Wharf Lighthouse, now part of the Salem Maritime National Historic Site. Salem is also home to the Marblehead Light, which shines from atop New England's only iron-skeleton navigational tower, and the Baker's Island Lighthouse, which played a key role in the War of 1812, when it helped save the famous frigate *Constitution*.

PORTSMOUTH HARBOR LIGHT

The Portsmouth Harbor Light had existed for only a few years when revolutionary fever swept through Massachusetts and Britain's other North American colonies. Located on what was then Fort William and Mary (now Fort Constitution), the new light station witnessed one of the first overt acts of rebellion against British rule in 1775, when local militia raided the fort and carried away its stocks of gunpowder. Barrels of this same black powder were later hauled south and put to use by Continental forces in the Battle of Bunker Hill.

Established in 1771, several years before the Revolution, the Portsmouth Harbor beacon has guided ships longer than all but a few lighthouses in North America. At first it consisted of nothing more than a lantern hung from a pole on the grounds of a fort. By 1784 the light shone from atop an 80-foot octagonal wooden tower, which eventually succumbed to rot and the concussions of the fort's mighty cannon. Rebuilt in 1804, it served until 1877, when the Lighthouse Service replaced it with a 48-foot cylindrical structure made of bolted iron plates. This lighthouse still stands, its fourth-order Fresnel lens shooting out a fixed-green beam visible from 12 miles away.

Over the years the Portsmouth Harbor Lighthouse has hosted many distinguished visitors, including General Lafayette, Daniel Webster, and Henry David Thoreau. But the most important—and likely the gruffest—personage to knock on the door here was President George Washington. He inspected the light station in 1789 and found its upkeep less than satisfactory. Not surprisingly, its keeper was summarily fired.

Location: Portsmouth, New Hampshire

Established: 1771

Tower height: 48 feet

Elevation of the focal plane: 52 feet

Optic: Fresnel lens (fourth order)

Status: Active

Characteristic: Fixed green

Range: 12 miles

Position: 43° 04' 18
70° 42' 30

Note: Scene of early Revolutionary War raid

TO SEE THE LIGHT: From U.S. Highway 1 or 1B in Portsmouth, follow signs to Fort Constitution. The nearby lighthouse is on an active Coast Guard base and at present off-limits to the public. However, the lighthouse can be enjoyed and photographed from the massive walls of the historic fort. As with many lighthouses, the best view of this one is likely from the water; contact Portsmouth Harbor Cruises at (800) 776-0915.

ISLES OF SHOALS LIGHT

The Isles of Shoals, consisting of a scatter of rocks a few miles east of Portsmouth, New Hampshire, have long attracted the adventurous and hardy of spirit. Barren, swept by high winds, and pounded on all sides by towering waves, the Isles of Shoals are more a part of the ocean than of the land. Yet this tiny archipelago—some of its islets no more than a few dozen yards across—was home to one of the earliest European settlements in North America. During the sixteenth century, fishermen flocked here like seabirds to exploit the giant schools of cod that teemed in the waters off the coast. Houses, churches, and packing sheds clung tenuously to the rocks. On more than a few occasions, Atlantic storms all but obliterated the tiny island community, forcing residents to rebuilt their shattered homes and lives.

During the mid-1800s Ralph Waldo Emerson visited the Appledore Hotel, a gracious hostelry located on one of the Isles of

Shoals' nine islands. Other guests included Nathaniel Hawthorne, William Mason, and John Greenleaf Whittier. The Old Appledore Hotel fell into ruin long ago, and all but a few traces of it are gone. Yet plenty of summer visitors still come. A research station operated by Cornell University and the University of New Hampshire draws students and scientists who study the unique environment and wildlife of the islands. There is also a nondenominational church camp operated by Unitarian-Universalists.

A lighthouse has stood on White Island—one of the Isles' more barren outcroppings—since 1821. The original stone tower soared eighty-two feet above the island and served until just before the Civil War. In 1859 it was replaced by a shorter brick tower, its walls built two feet thick to help them survive the Atlantic's pounding waves. Often, prodigious storms have struck the island, their thundering surf driving keepers into the tower for refuge. Today the station is uninhabited, its automated light powered with batteries recharged by solar panels.

Exposed to frequent gales, the old lighthouse has deteriorated markedly since the light was automated in 1987. New Hampshire elementary school children are helping raise money to restore the tower and other buildings.

TO SEE THE LIGHT: White Island is off-limits to the general public, but the station can be seen from the water and from adjacent islands. Portsmouth-based tour boats offer excursions to the historic Isles of Shoals as well as special lighthouse cruises featuring the Portsmouth Harbor Lighthouse and several other scenic light towers in nearby Maine. For information call the Isles of Shoals Steamship Company at (603) 431–5500 or Portsmouth Harbor Cruises at (800) 776–0915.

Location: Off Portsmouth, New Hampshire

Established: 1821

Tower height: 58 feet

Elevation of the focal plane: 82 feet

Optic: Modern (solar powered)

Status: Active

Characteristic: Flashes white every 15 seconds

Range: 20 miles

Position: 42° 58' 00
70° 37' 24

Note: A haunt of literary giants

NEWBURYPORT HARBOR LIGHT

stablished in 1788 at about the time the U.S. Constitution was ratified, the Newburyport Harbor Light is one of America's oldest navigational beacons. The original station consisted of two lights displayed from a pair of towers erected by a local business and civic organization known as the Newburyport Marine Society. The lights were intended to guide freighters into the Merrimack River and, so, increase local commerce.

Shirin Pagels

During the 1790s the U.S. government took charge of the
nation's maritime beacons, including those at Newburyport. Over the
next two centuries, the station was altered and refurbished so often
that little or nothing of the original remains. The existing Newburyport
Harbor Lighthouse, located on Plum Island near the entrance to the
river, dates to 1898. A 45-foot wood structure topped by an iron
lantern still functions, alerting mariners with a green occulting light
focused by a classic fourth-order Fresnel lens.

Although relatively quiet today, Plum Island was a popular
resort in the nineteenth century. During the summer droves of tourists
arrived in Newburyport by train or steamship and took the trolley out
to the island beaches. Nowadays, however, Newburyport is better
known for its museums and other historic attractions.

The Newburyport Harbor Lighthouse (also called Plum Island
Light) is historically notable both for its considerable age and for
the fact that this was the first American light station to employ
Argand lamps. These clean-burning, mostly smoke-free oil lamps fed
a stream of air to the flame through a tube and used a hollow wick
to produce an exceptionally intense light. The brainchild of French
inventor Francois-Pierre-Ami Argand, they were introduced to
European lighthouses during the late eighteenth century, but not
widely used in America until much later. When the Newburyport
station was refurbished in 1809, it was equipped with Argand
lamps.

TO SEE THE LIGHT: From U.S. Highway 1 in Newburyport, follow
Route 1A and then Ocean Avenue onto Plum Island. The lighthouse
is on the south end of the island in the Parker River National Wildlife
Refuge (978–465–5753). The grounds are open all year; the light-
house has occasional open houses. The Newburyport Harbor
Lighthouse is owned by the City of Newburyport and leased to the
Friends of Plum Island, which can be reached at P.O. Box 381,
Newburyport, MA 01950.

While in the area, don't miss the Custom House Maritime
Museum on Water Street in Newburyport; call (978) 462–8681.
Among the featured exhibits is a fourth-order Fresnel lens similar to
the one at the Newburyport Harbor Light. Not far from the museum
is the old Newburyport Front Range tower (see next page) that at
one time helped guide ships into the harbor.

Location: Newburyport,
Massachusetts

Established: 1788

Tower height: 45 feet

Elevation of the focal
plane: 50 feet

Optic: Fresnel
(fourth order)

Status: Active

Characteristic: Green
occulting twice every
15 seconds

Range: 10 miles

Position: 42° 48' 54
70° 49' 06

Note: First American use
of Argand oil lamps

NEWBURYPORT RANGE LIGHT TOWERS

The Newburyport Rear Range tower and its Front Range companion tower reflected in an office window. Shirin Pagels

Location: Newburyport

Established: 1873

Tower height: 53 feet (rear) 15 feet (front)

Status: Deactivated in 1961

Note: Early use of range light system

Narrow channels must be carefully navigated or else a vessel is likely to strike a shoal or run aground in the shallows. Range lights are intended to help mariners steer a straight course and avoid these perils. A range light system consists of two separate beacons placed one behind the other. A helmsman can safely navigate a channel by keeping the lights in vertical alignment. One of the earliest uses of such a system came in 1873 at Newburyport, where a pair of lights marked the Merrimack River entrance. The rear-range light was displayed from a 53-foot, square, brick tower just upriver from Bailey's Wharf. A smaller, cylindrical, cast-iron tower located on the wharf itself provided the front-range light. The Newburyport Range Lights served mariners until 1961. Both structures still exist, but the smaller front-range tower has been removed from the wharf and placed on the grounds of the Newburyport Coast Guard station.

TO SEE THE LIGHTS: The rear-range tower is located on Water Street in Newburyport. To visit the front-range tower you must ask permission to enter the nearby Coast Guard facility. As is the case with many lighthouses, the best way to see these towers is from the water. Harbor cruises offer an excellent view of the lighthouses and plenty of interesting historical tidbits; call (888) 975–1842.

ANNISQUAM HARBOR LIGHT

Wigwam Point got its name because Native Americans camped here during the early colonial era, most likely to take advantage of the fine local fishing. The wigwams were only a memory by 1801, when the government established a light station on the point to guide local fishermen into port. The station's first two towers lasted about half a century each. The first, a small wooden structure, slowly rotted over the years and was finally replaced by a larger structure in 1851. The existing 41-foot tower dates to 1897, and it was built to last. Its fortress-like brick walls are 4-feet thick at the base. Perhaps not surprisingly, this tower still stands and continues to serve mariners. Its flashing light warns vessels away from the dangerous Squam Bar near the mouth of the Annisquam River.

TO SEE THE LIGHT: From Route 127 in Annisquam, follow Lane Road, Elizabeth Road, Ocean Avenue, and Harraden Circle to Wigwam Road. Then turn onto Lighthouse Road and follow it to the station. Still managed by the Coast Guard, the station property is off-limits to the public, but the lighthouse can be seen from the gate. Summer cruises from Gloucester make it possible to enjoy this and other area lighthouses from the water; call (978) 768–7037.

Location: Near Rockport

Established: 1801

Tower height: 45 feet

Elevation of the focal plane: 41 feet

Optic: Modern

Status: Active

Characteristic: Flashes white every 7.5 seconds (red sector)

Range: 14 miles

Position: 42° 39' 42
70° 40' 54

Note: Also known as Wigwam Point Lighthouse

Shirin Pagels

STRAITSMOUTH ISLAND LIGHT

Location: Near Rockport

Established: 1835

Tower height: 37 feet

Elevation of the focal
plane: 46 feet

Optic: Modern
(solar powered)

Status: Active

Characteristic: Flashes
green every 6 seconds

Range: 6 miles

Position: 42° 39' 42
70° 35' 18

Note: Now part of a
wildlife sanctuary

L ocated on Straitsmouth Island just off Cape Ann, this still-active maritime light has marked the entrance to Rockport Harbor since 1835. The original brick tower was replaced in 1850 by a taller stone structure, which gave way in 1896 to the existing brick lighthouse. Interestingly enough, the old 1835, wood, keeper's residence still stands but has fallen into an extreme state of disrepair. Some think the old dwelling may not outlast the next big storm, and it has been placed on *Lighthouse Digest's* "Doomsday List." Although exposed to regular pounding by the mounting waves of Atlantic gales, the tower itself remains sturdy.

TO SEE THE LIGHT: The lighthouse can be seen from Bearskin Neck in Rockport, but the best view is from the water. For information on summer lighthouse cruises that pass by this and several other lighthouses in the Gloucester/Rockport area, call (978) 768-7037. The Thacher Island Association also offers occasional lighthouse excursions that provide a view of the Straitsmouth Island Lighthouse; call (978) 546-7697.

Shirin Pagels

For more than 170 years, the Eastern Point beacon has guided Gloucester fishermen safely home from the sea. The tower and dwelling stand on the east side of the town's harbor on a long, rocky point of land that forms a natural breakwater. In 1832 the federal government built a modest stone tower near the end of the point, equipping it with an array of whale-oil lamps and parabolic reflectors. The light was intended to do double duty by guiding vessels to Gloucester and warning them away from a dangerous obstacle near the harbor entrance known as Dog Bar Reef.

In 1848 a second, larger, stone tower replaced the original structure. The 36-foot brick tower that guards the point today dates to 1890. The fourth-order Fresnel lens that focused the station's beacon for more than a century was replaced by a modern optic in 1994.

TO SEE THE LIGHT: The light station is located at the end of Eastern Point Boulevard in East Gloucester. A stone breakwater extending nearly half a mile from the end of the point offers the best viewing. The cast-iron Ten Pound Island Lighthouse tower and its flashing red light can be seen from the same breakwater. For cruises passing these historic lighthouses, contact the Friends of the Boston Harbor Islands at (781) 740–4290 or the Thacher Island Association at (978) 546–7697.

Location: Gloucester

Established: 1832

Tower height: 36 feet

Elevation of the focal plane: 57 feet

Optic: Modern

Status: Active

Characteristic: Flashes white every 5 seconds

Range: 24 miles

Position: 42° 34' 49
70° 39' 52

Note: Marks dangerous Dog Bar Reef

CAPE ANN LIGHTS

A mong the oldest and most historic light stations in America, the twin Cape Ann Lights on barren Thacher Island first beamed out their warnings in 1771, several years before the signing of the Declaration of Independence. During the Revolutionary War, the lights were snuffed out to prevent their use by British warships. Fortunately for the countless mariners whose lives have been saved by the Cape Ann beacons over the years, the lamps were relit soon after the war ended.

Occasionally, lighthouse keepers have been saved by their own lights. On Christmas Eve 1865, the assistant keeper at Cape Ann fell seriously ill. The station's keeper, a disabled Civil War veteran named Bray, felt he had no choice but to take the sick man to the mainland, where he could receive proper medical attention. While Bray was ashore, the sea was brewing a storm. When the keeper headed back to Thacher Island in his small boat, he found himself rowing into the teeth of a blizzard. It was snowing so hard that Bray had no idea whether he was pulling toward the island or toward the open sea. To miss the island meant almost certain death, and for a time Bray thought that was exactly what he had done. Then he saw the glow of two familiar lights. His wife and children had struggled through deep snowdrifts to keep the lamps burning. Bray pointed his boat toward the lights and put his back into the oars. Later, sitting at the table in his warm house and surrounded by his family, the keeper may have thought he had never tasted such a good Christmas dinner.

No less thankful to the Cape Ann Lights was Woodrow Wilson, whose second term as president might have ended early if not for

their timely warning. While carrying Wilson home from the 1919 Versailles peace conference that officially ended World War I, the passenger liner *America* got caught in a dense fog off the Massachusetts coast. With the great liner plowing blindly toward the rocks of Thacher Island, the *America*'s helmsman heard the Cape Ann foghorn and caught the glimmer of the lights just in time to turn away and prevent disaster.

The two 124-foot granite towers that stood on Thacher Island in 1919 and still stand there now are not the originals. They date from 1861, when they replaced a pair of much smaller towers built almost a century earlier. The north light was taken out of service during the 1920s after the government discontinued use of multiple-light beacons. Recently, however, the old north tower was restored and relit for historical reasons, and the station once more displays its distinctive double lights. The enormous first-order Fresnel lenses that formerly served here were removed in 1932.

TO SEE THE LIGHTS: Thacher Island is accessible only by boat, but you can see the towers from Route 127A near Rockport on Cape Ann. For information on occasional summer lighthouse cruises or excursions to Thacher Island, contact the Thacher Island Association, P.O. Box 73, Rockport, MA 01966; (978) 546–7697.

Location: Thacher Island

Established: 1771

Tower height: 124 feet

Elevation of the focal plane: 166 feet

Optic: Modern (solar powered)

Status: Active

Characteristic: Flashes red every 5 seconds

Range: 17 miles

Position: 42° 38' 12
70° 34' 30

Note: America's first twin-towered light station

TEN POUND ISLAND LIGHT

Having guided generations of mariners into Gloucester's harbor, the Ten Pound Island Lighthouse recently became a movie star in addition to a navigational beacon. It was featured prominently in the hit action thriller *The Perfect Storm*, released in 2000, but has been in "pictures" before. Noted artist Winslow Homer painted here during the early 1880s.

Ten Pound Island Light has marked Gloucester Harbor for the better part of two centuries. A 40-foot stone tower, wood-frame dwelling, and several outbuildings were constructed on the island in 1821. Sixty years later, the original tower was replaced by a 30-foot-tall, cast-iron cylinder lined with brick. A fifth-order Fresnel lens served here until 1956, when the Coast Guard deactivated the light. Thanks to the efforts of local citizens and the Lighthouse Preservation Society, the beacon returned to service in 1989. It remains in operation, but nowadays its light is focused by a modern optic.

TO SEE THE LIGHT: The lighthouse and its beacon can be seen from the breakwater extending from Eastern Point in Gloucester. Ferries and harbor cruises offer close-up views of the tower; call the Gloucester Chamber of Commerce at (978) 283–1601. Additional cruise options are offered by the Friends of the Boston Harbor Islands at (781) 740–4290 or the Thacher Island Association at (978) 546–7697.

Location: Gloucester

Established: 1821

Tower height: 30 feet

Elevation of the focal plane: 57 feet

Optic: Modern

Status: Active

Characteristic: Red for 6 seconds, then dark for 6 seconds

Range: 5 miles

Position: 42° 36' 06 70° 39' 54

Note: Winslow Homer painted here

Shirin Pagels

BAKER'S ISLAND LIGHT

Although not one of America's so-called "colonial lights," the Baker's Island Lighthouse is nonetheless venerable. Established in 1798 during the administration of John Adams, America's second president, the station originally displayed two beacons. The lighthouse consisted of two separate towers connected to a central keeper's dwelling. As an economy measure, one light was deactivated in 1870 and its tower torn down. The remaining 59-foot-tall granite tower has survived, its lantern still displaying alternating red and white lights. A pair of Victorian-style keeper's dwellings, built in 1878, stand nearby.

Like most lighthouses, the one on Baker's Island has saved its share of ships, but few of them were as important to the nation as the USS *Constitution*. During the War of 1812, Baker's Island keeper Joseph Perkins watched proudly as the *Constitution* sailed along the Massachusetts coast toward Salem. Then he spotted a pair of large British warships bearing down on the famous American frigate. Outnumbered and outgunned, the captain of the *Constitution* wanted to avoid a battle and hoped to slip inside the harbor, where shore guns could drive away the British. Unable to find a safe channel into the harbor, the captain turned to the lighthouse for assistance. A former ship's pilot, Perkins rowed out to the *Constitution*, took over at the helm, and steered "Old Ironsides" into Salem Harbor.

TO SEE THE LIGHT: The lighthouse can be seen from Harbor Street or Boardman Avenue, off Route 127 in Manchester-by-the-Sea. For cruises passing this lighthouse, contact the Friends of the Boston Harbor Islands at (781) 740–4290 or Sun Line, Ltd. at (978) 741–1900.

Shirin Pagels

Location: Manchester-by-the-Sea

Established: 1798

Tower height: 59 feet

Elevation of the focal plane: 111 feet

Optic: Modern (solar powered)

Status: Active

Characteristic: Alternates red and white at 20-second intervals

Range: 16 miles

Position: 42° 33' 11
70° 47' 09

Note: Originally displayed two lights

HOSPITAL POINT LIGHT

O nce known as Paul's Point, the strategic promontory northeast of Salem became Hospital Point after a clinic was built there in 1801 to treat victims of a smallpox epidemic. The clinic burned in 1849 and the epidemic was mercifully forgotten by the early 1870s, when the U.S. Lighthouse Board selected Hospital Point as the site of an important navigational station. Completed in 1872, the lighthouse was assigned the task of guiding vessels through the narrow Salem harbor entrance channel.

Although Hospital point was not considered a major seacoast light station, it received a relatively powerful third-order Fresnel lens, which remains in use to this day. The lens is of unusual design: It contains a "condensing panel," or vertical magnifying lens that intensifies the light seen from ships in the middle of the channel; the light dims if the vessel begins to stray.

To mark the channel even more efficiently, the station was converted for use as a range light in 1927. The original lighthouse on Hospital Point became the front-range beacon, while an automated optic placed in a church spire about a mile away provided the rear-range light. Both lights remain in service.

TO SEE THE LIGHTS:

Located in Beverly at the end of Bayview Avenue, the Hospital Point Lighthouse is an active Coast Guard facility and not open to the public. The tower and adjacent residence can be seen from nearby Lynch Park, but the best views are from the water. The Friends of the Boston Harbor Islands offers occasional cruises that pass this lighthouse and several others; call (781) 740–4290. The Hospital Point Rear-Range Light shines from Beverly's two-century-old First Baptist Church on Church Street.

Location: Beverly

Established: 1872

Tower height: 45 feet

Elevation of the focal plane: 70 feet

Optic: Fresnel lens (third order)

Status: Active

Characteristic: Fixed white

Range: 12 miles

Position: 42° 32' 48
            70° 51' 24

Note: Rear-range light shines from a nearby church steeple

Shirin Pagels

Location: Winter Island, Salem Harbor

Established: 1871

Tower height: 32 feet

Elevation of the focal plane: 28 feet

Optic: Modern (solar powered)

Status: Private aid to navigation

Characteristic: Flashes every 4 seconds

Range: 4 miles

Position: 42° 31' 36 70° 52' 00

Note: Stands beside a seventeenth-century fort

During the nineteenth century Salem was one of America's most prosperous ports, and freighters were guided to the city's bustling wharves by an impressive array of maritime lights. Among these were the Baker's Island and Marblehead Lights to the east, the Hospital Point Range Lights in Beverly, and the Derby Wharf Light in Salem harbor itself. All these lights can still be seen from Winter Island where yet another old lighthouse marks the harbor entrance. The latter historic tower stands just outside the ruined walls of Fort Pickering, an old stone bastion dating back to the 1640s.

A conical cast-iron tower with a black lantern, the Fort Pickering Lighthouse guided mariners from 1872 until 1969, when the Coast Guard deactivated its light. Some years later local sailors and businesses formed the Fort Pickering Light Association and raised enough money to restore the historic tower. In 1983 its beacon was relit as a private aid to navigation.

TO SEE THE LIGHT: Winter Island can be reached from the mainland via Winter Island Road, which will take you to Fort Pickering and its lighthouse. The Winter Island Maritime Park on the island features the tiny Fort Pickering Lighthouse. The park also provides views of several other lighthouses in the Salem area; call (978) 745–9430.

DERBY WHARF LIGHT

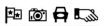

Location: Salem

Established: 1870

Tower height: 23 feet

Elevation of the focal plane: 25 feet

Optic: Modern (solar powered)

Status: Private aid to navigation

Characteristic: Flashes red every 6 seconds

Range: 4 miles

Position: 42° 30' 59
70° 53' 01

Note: Derby Wharf is named for America's first millionaire

N owadays, Salem is perhaps most widely known for its infamous seventeenth-century witch trials, but that was not always the case. Clipper ship captains once fondly regarded Salem as the "Venice of the New World." This vibrant New England port city sent large fleets of merchant ships to India, China, and the West Indies. When these "Indiamen" returned, sizable fortunes were made on the spices, sugar, molasses, coffee, tea, and chinaware that poured out of their holds. The largest of these fortunes was accumulated by Elias Derby, an importer whose razor sharp business acumen made him America's first millionaire. Although not a seaman himself, Derby knew how to make money on shipping ventures, and he swelled his profits by investing in construction of the enormous wharf that now bears his name.

Derby Wharf had stood for a century before government maritime officials decided to mark it with a lighthouse. Construction of the simple, 12-foot-square brick tower was completed during fall 1870 and its whale lamps lit early the following year. Only 23 feet tall, the diminutive Derby Wharf Light was no giant, but it served its purpose well, guiding freighters to the Salem wharves until 1977, when the light was deactivated. In 1983 the National Park Service and a local preservation group called Friends of Salem Maritime relit the Derby Wharf beacon in celebration of the city's extraordinary maritime heritage.

TO SEE THE LIGHT: Old Salem, with its fascinating cemeteries, museums, shops, wharf, and lighthouse, is located off Highway 1A. The lighthouse is in a small park at the end of the wharf off Derby Street. Nearby is the official visitor center for the Salem Maritime National Historic Site, a treasury of structures dating back as far as the seventeenth century. For more information write to Salem Maritime National Historic Site, 193 Derby Street, Salem, MA 01970 or call (978) 740–1660.

MARBLEHEAD LIGHT

Development has been an enemy of lighthouses. Newly constructed seaside hotels and other tall buildings have obscured beacons, forcing officials to move or even discontinue some light stations. Among the first lighthouses to be walled in by adjacent buildings was the small harbor light on Marblehead near Salem. Built in 1836 for $4,500, the squat Marblehead tower was not much taller than an ordinary house. It served effectively for many years, but by 1880 large summer cottages had sprouted like weeds all around the station, making it all but impossible for helmsmen trying to steer their vessels into Salem Harbor to see the light.

Location: Marblehead

Established: 1836

Tower height: 105 feet

Elevation of the focal plane: 130 feet

Optic: Modern

Status: Active

Characteristic: Fixed green

Range: 7 miles

Position: 42° 30' 18
70° 50' 00

Note: Only steel-skeleton light tower in New England

As a temporary remedy, the keeper anchored a 100-foot mast firmly in the ground, and each night he hoisted a lantern to the top. Eventually, this inadequate arrangement drew so many complaints from sailors that the Lighthouse Board approved a new tower for Marblehead. By 1895 work crews had completed the structure, a skeleton tower poised on eight iron legs. With its lantern 105 feet above the ground and 130 feet above the harbor, it raised the light far above the cottages that besieged the old lighthouse.

The station was automated in 1960 after more than 115 years in the care of tough, hardworking lighthouse keepers. The first was Ezekiel Darling, a former gunner on the USS *Constitution* who served at Marblehead for twenty-five years. Jane Martin took over from Darling in 1860 and was, at the time, the only female lighthouse keeper in New England. Among the last Marblehead keepers was Harry Marden, a man who knew how to handle an emergency. During the great New England Hurricane of 1938, the station's electric power failed, so Marden drove his car to the tower, hooked cables to the battery, and kept the light burning.

TO SEE THE LIGHT: In Marblehead follow Ocean Avenue across a causeway onto Marblehead Neck. After the causeway bear left onto Harbor Avenue, and then follow Ocean Avenue and Follett Street to a parking area near the lighthouse. A small park here provides an excellent view of both the Marblehead tower and the Baker's Island Light offshore. It's also a great place to enjoy a gorgeous sunset.

EGG ROCK LIGHT

Many of America's "Lost Lights" were destroyed by storm, fire, or rot, and more than a few have fallen to explosions or a wrecker's crane; but none came to a more ignominious end than the Egg Rock Lighthouse. Built in 1897, it replaced an earlier structure that had marked the rock since 1856. During the 1920s, the government sold the old keeper's dwelling for a mere $5.00, but it was evident from the first that the new owners would have difficulty collecting their property. In 1927 they lifted the dwelling off its foundation with jacks and tried to lower it onto a barge so they could move it to the mainland. During this process a rope broke and the lighthouse plunged into the sea.

Location: Near Lynn Beach and Nahant Beach

Established: 1856

Tower height: 32 feet

Elevation of the focal plane: 90 feet

Optic: Modern (solar powered)

Status: Destroyed in 1927

Note: Keeper's house fell into the sea

CHAPTER TWO:
BOSTON TO PLYMOUTH

Established in 1716, the Boston Light shines at the very heart of America's colonial and Revolutionary War history. Some of the dramatic events related to that history are recounted in the introduction to this book. However, the old harbor sentinel is not the only Boston-area maritime beacon with a fascinating past.

Although not nearly so old as its venerable neighbor on Little Brewster Island, the Graves Ledge Lighthouse near the northern entrance to Boston Harbor has seen more than its share of drama. Completed in 1905, the open-water granite tower has stood up to countless gales. In January 1941 an especially powerful blizzard rolled over the harbor, driving the freighter *Mary O'Hara* into a barge anchored near the station. As the fatally stricken *O'Hara* sank, her crew of nineteen scrambled into the rigging. Unable to render assistance, the Graves Ledge keeper was forced to watch as one by one the freezing sailors lost their grip, fell into the icy surf, and were carried out to sea by the tide.

Nearly a century earlier, in fall 1849, a similar storm had swept in out of the Atlantic, pushing the *Saint John*, a crowded passenger ship, onto Minots Ledge southeast of Boston. Lurking just beneath the waves at high tide, this lethal obstacle had already run up a grim toll of shattered vessels and drowned passengers and crew, but this would be the most deadly wreck of them all, with about one hundred drowned. Battered incessantly by enormous waves, the *Saint John* soon broke apart, dumping her load of Irish immigrants into the sea. For days afterward, their bloated bodies washed up on the beaches near Cohasset.

Strangely enough, the wreck took place practically in the shadow of an as-yet-unfinished lighthouse being built directly over the ledge. An experimental structure, it was an open-walled, iron-skeleton tower with eight legs anchored to the subsurface rock. Completed and ready for duty in early 1850, only a few weeks after the loss of the *Saint John*, the Minots Ledge Lighthouse stood for less than fifteen months before it, too, succumbed to a gale. During the early morning darkness of March 17, 1851, a mighty storm swept over the Massachusetts coast and grew in intensity until waves were climbing the Minots Ledge tower. At first the structure withstood the fierce pounding, but soon its legs began to buckle. Finally, the tower groaned and fell into the ocean, carrying keepers Joseph Antoine and Joseph Wilson to their deaths. Observers on the nearby mainland watched in horror as the tragedy unfolded, and some reported that Antoine and Wilson kept the light burning until the last instant.

This disaster was to have a profound effect on lighthouse history. Up until that time maritime lights in America had been administered by Treasury Department bureaucrats the likes of Stephen J. Pleasonton, a parsimonious auditor with no experience in either navigation or engineering. During an autocratic, thirty-year reign over the U.S. Lighthouse Service, Pleasonton consistently emphasized economy at the expense of quality when letting contracts for lighthouse equipment, materials, and construction. He also resisted innovations such as the sophisticated but expensive French-made Fresnel lenses that might have saved countless ships and lives. But despite his resistance to new ideas—especially if they were costly—Pleasonton had approved the experimental tower at Minots Ledge. Ironically, this uncharacteristic willingness to try fresh technology was destined to cost him his job.

As it turned out, the disaster at Minots Ledge focused the attention of Congress on Pleasonton's poor administrative record. Alarmed by a rapidly growing list of maritime calamities, Congress convened an investigative commission, and its report, delivered in spring 1851, was distinctly unflattering. Everywhere it looked, the commission found lighthouses with cracked and crumbling walls, outmoded lamps, and inferior optics. Sea captains told commissioners that some American beacons were so weak that ships ran aground while looking for them. Congress responded by taking the Lighthouse Service away from Pleasonton—he was never actually fired—and placing it in the hands of a Lighthouse Board consisting largely of military men, engineers, and sailors. In time the board succeeded in modernizing a lighthouse system that in many ways had changed little since colonial times.

Among the most historic of the navigational stations that have served mariners since the colonial era is the one near Plymouth, where the Pilgrims made landfall in 1620. The Pilgrims stepped ashore in safety largely because their vessel, the *Mayflower*, was able to anchor in calm waters sheltered by a fish-shaped strip of land now known as the Gurnet. About 150 years later this strategic peninsula would be marked by a lighthouse, only the sixth built in all of what is now the United States and among the first to display two lights. The old lighthouse still guides mariners but nowadays

Location: Boston

Established: 1905

Tower height: 113 feet

Elevation of the focal plane: 98 feet

Optic: Modern (solar powered)

Status: Active

Characteristic: Flashes white twice every 12 seconds

Range: 15 miles

Position: 42° 21' 54 70° 52' 09

Note: Named for Thomas Graves, a famous colonial clipper ship captain

ray and weather-streaked, the stone tower guarding Graves Ledge looks very old but dates only from 1905, making it a relatively young lighthouse. Some think the ledge received its rather ominous name because of tragedies such as the one that befell the schooner *Mary O'Hara* in 1941. (During a blinding blizzard in January of that year, the unlucky vessel rammed a barge and sank, leaving nineteen of her crew to drown or freeze.) Actually, the ledge is named for Thomas Graves, a prominent colonial Massachusetts sea trader.

Built with interlocking granite blocks, the massive 113-foot tower easily turns aside even the largest storm-driven waves. The lighthouse was automated in 1976, and its huge, first-order Fresnel lens was exchanged for a modern lens. Seen from up to 25 miles at sea, the flashing white light is almost as powerful as that of the Boston Light on nearby Little Brewster Island.

TO SEE THE LIGHT: For cruises that offer close-up water views of Boston Light, Graves Ledge Light, and Long Island Head Light, contact Boston Harbor Explorers at (617) 479–1871, Bay State Cruises at (617) 457–1428, or Boston Harbor Cruises at (617) 227–4321.

LONG ISLAND HEAD LIGHT

The Boston Light had shined for more than a century by the time government maritime authorities decided to give the city a second light station. In 1819 a lighthouse was built on the seaward tip of the long, narrow island that nearly bisects Boston's outer harbor. A modest stone tower equipped with oil lamps, the Long Island Head Light was intended to mark President Roads, a key channel linking the harbor to the open Atlantic.

In 1844 the station's original tower was replaced by a cast-iron structure, the first of its kind in America. The new and, at that time, experimental tower consisted of iron plates bolted together to form a 34-foot cylinder topped by an iron lantern. The experiment proved a success, and durable iron soon became a popular construction material for lighthouses, especially those in exposed locations. Many iron lighthouses still mark important points along the U.S. coast, but the Long Island Head is not one of them. In 1901 the tower was removed to make room for a harbor bastion, and a new brick lighthouse was built outside the fortress walls.

Still an active maritime beacon and Coast Guard facility, the Long Island Head Light Station is off-limits to the public, though apparently not to ghosts. The island and its lighthouse are said to be haunted by a "scarlet lady" who, according to legend, was the wife of a British soldier killed there during the Revolutionary War.

TO SEE THE LIGHT: For cruises that offer close-up water views of Boston Light, Graves Ledge Light, and Long Island Head Light, contact Boston Harbor Explorers at (617) 479–1871, Bay State Cruises at (617) 457–1428, or Boston Harbor Cruises at (617) 227–4321.

Location: Boston

Established: 1819

Tower height: 52 feet

Elevation of the focal plane: 120 feet

Optic: Modern

Status: Active

Characteristic: Flashes white every 2.5 seconds

Range: 6 miles

Position: 42° 19' 48
70° 57' 30

Note: Nation's first cast-iron lighthouse

Shirin Pagels

BOSTON LIGHT

The oldest navigational station in all of North America, Boston Light is a national treasure. Built in 1716 on Little Brewster Island—it was known as Beacon Island during the eighteenth century—at the entrance to the harbor, it helped attract the fleets of trading ships that made Boston one of the world's most prosperous cities. Its light had been shining for almost sixty years by the time Paul Revere saw a different sort of beacon in the belfry of Boston's Old North Church and hurried off on his famous ride. The lighthouse was destroyed by the British during the Revolutionary War but was rebuilt in 1783.

The post-Revolutionary tower still stands and its light continues to guide ships more than two centuries after it was built. The tower's extraordinary longevity is no accident. Aware the lighthouse could face other wars, not to mention fierce battles with Atlantic storms, the Boston masons who built the 1783 tower gave it fortress-like walls more than 7 feet thick at the base. In 1853 its height was raised by 15 feet and its stone walls lined with brick. Otherwise, except for reinforcing steel hoops added in 1983, the tower remains essentially unchanged.

Nearly as venerable as the tower itself is the second-order Fresnel lens installed here in 1859. It remains in service, producing a flashing white light visible from an impressive distance of more than 27 miles at sea. Although the light was automated in 1998, the Coast Guard maintains an active station on the island.

Despite the great power of the station's light and the strength of its fog signals, a number of ships have been lost practically within shouting distance of the lighthouse. In December 1839 three hurricanes struck Boston Harbor in less than two weeks, wrecking scores of vessels and driving the schooner *Charlotte* and the bark *Lloyd* onto rocks near the light. In 1861 the 991-ton square-rigger *Maritana* got caught in a blinding snowstorm in Massachusetts Bay and slammed into Shag Rocks, a short distance from Boston Light; dozens drowned or were crushed to death when the big wooden ship broke in half. Using a small dory, lighthouse personnel rescued twelve survivors who had floated to Shag Rocks on fragments of the ship. In 1882 the Shag Rocks also claimed the *Fanny Pike*, but the keeper managed to rescue the entire crew.

The schooner *Calvin F. Baker* hit rocks and sank near the lighthouse during a storm in 1898. Before help could arrive, three crewmen froze to death in the rigging. On Christmas Day 1909, the coal schooner *Davis Palmer* slammed into Finn's Ledge and went

Location: Boston Harbor

Established: 1716

Tower height: 89 feet

Elevation of the focal plane: 102 feet

Optic: Fresnel (second order)

Status: Active

Characteristic: Flashes white every 10 seconds

Range: 27 miles

Position: 42° 19' 42
70° 53' 24

Note: Oldest light station in America

down with all hands. Fate was kinder to the crew of the USS *Alacrity*, a Navy ship that hit rocks just off Little Brewster Island on February 3, 1918. The *Alacrity* sank, but its twenty-four half-frozen crewmen were rescued by keeper Charles Jennings, who had to push his dory over ice and through freezing surf to reach them.

TO SEE THE LIGHT: Little Brewster Island is part of Boston Harbor Islands State Park. The Friends of the Boston Harbor Islands offers occasional excursions to Little Brewster Island with visits to the lighthouse; call (781) 740–4290. For close-up water views of Boston Light, Graves Ledge Light, and Long Island Head Light, contact Boston Harbor Explorers at (617) 479–1871, Bay State Cruises at (617) 457–1428, or Boston Harbor Cruises at (617) 227–4321. Airliners landing at Boston's Logan Airport offer thrilling views of these historic light stations.

Established: 1856

Tower height: 35 feet

Elevation of the focal
plane: 35 feet

Status: Destroyed by
fire in 1929

Note: Known to locals
as "Bug Light"

NARROWS LIGHT

When seen from a distance, the Narrows Lighthouse seemed to hover over the shimmering harbor like some sort of long-legged insect. Bostonians spoke of it affectionately as the "Bug Light," and for generations it guided vessels safely around the sandy shallows on the landward side of Great Brewster Island.

Built in 1856, it was a cottage-style, screw-pile lighthouse, consisting of a modest, eight-sided wooden building resting on a small forest of cast-iron legs. Many lighthouses of this type were built during the nineteenth century in the Chesapeake Bay and similar stretches of protected water in the South, but over the years most gave way to sturdier structures. Since they were vulnerable to ice, screw-pile lighthouses were rarely seen in the north, and Boston's "Bug Light" was the only ever built in New England. In 1929 the Narrows Lighthouse was destroyed in a fire that started when the keeper tried to burn faded paint off the walls with a blowtorch.

Bug Light, Boston Harbor, Mass.

Few navigational obstacles have snuffed out as many lives as Minots Ledge, a vicious shoal lurking just beneath the waves off Cohasset. Dozens of ships and countless smaller vessels wrecked on the ledge before anyone seriously considered marking the wave-swept shoal with a light. Finally, in 1850, Lighthouse Service crews completed an iron-skeleton tower, built on pilings hammered directly into the subsurface rock. Thought able to withstand any Atlantic storm, the tower stood for less than a year before a gale knocked it down, killing two assistant keepers.

The tower built in 1860 to take its place still stands, however. Its massive granite blocks dovetail, interlocking in such a way that the enormous pressures exerted on the walls by storm-driven waves actually strengthen them. Consisting of more than 1,000 carefully shaped blocks, the tower weighs more than 2,300 tons.

Automated in 1947, the tower lost its second-order Fresnel lens but not its unique one/one-two-three-four/one-two-three flashing sequence. Imaginative Cohasset folks read the flashes as I/L-O-V-E/Y-O-U and have given the Minots beacon the nickname "Lover's Light."

TO SEE THE LIGHT: The Minots Ledge tower and "Lover's Light" can be seen from beaches off Atlantic Avenue in Cohasset. For cruises that may pass within site of the tower see the Boston Harbor Lighthouse travel information. Although the lighthouse is off-limits to the public, you can visit the Minots Ledge Monument on Government Island in Cohasset Harbor. A near-exact replica of the Minots Ledge lantern room, it contains a Fresnel lens that was once used at the lighthouse as well as a memorial to the keepers who lost their lives when the first tower collapsed in 1851; for more information call (781) 383–6930. The Cohasset Maritime Museum on Elm Street features fascinating exhibits on the lighthouse; call (781) 383–6930.

Location: Cohasset

Established: 1850

Tower height: 97 feet

Elevation of the focal plane: 85 feet

Optic: Modern (solar powered)

Status: Active

Characteristic: Group flashing (1-4-3) every 45 seconds

Range: 10 miles

Position: 42° 16' 12
70° 45' 30

Note: Original tower & two keepers lost in a storm

In 1811 the government placed a light station at Scituate consisting of a small, wooden keeper's residence and a stone tower with sloped octagonal walls. The station's light was meant to guide ships into harbor and mark the deadly ledges near Cohasset, but it never performed the latter service adequately. Ships continued to wreck off Cohasset, which led to the construction of the Minots Ledge Lighthouse. Rendered obsolete by the offshore beacon, the Scituate light was retired in 1860.

Fortunately for lighthouse lovers and history buffs, the old Scituate tower and dwelling somehow survived many years of neglect. Eventually acquired by the Town of Scituate for use as a historical monument, the station has been attractively restored. In 1991, after more than 130 years in the dark, the lantern room was brightened by a modern optic, and its beacon returned to service as a private aid to navigation.

The Scituate Light serves as a reminder not just of the station's earlier service to mariners but also of a heroic stand made by the "Scituate Army of Two" during the War of 1812. Near the end of the war a British frigate landed a raiding party near the lighthouse. Keeper Simeon Bates was away at the time, but his two daughters proved more than a match for the British. Hidden from the raiders, they played a fife and drum with such exuberance that the redcoats imagined they were about to be attacked by militia and beat a hasty retreat.

TO SEE THE LIGHT: From Scituate Center follow the signs to Scituate Harbor. This will take you along First Parrish Road and Beaverdam Road to a left turn onto Hatherly Road. Bear right at Jericho Road, then turn onto Lighthouse Road and follow it to the lighthouse parking area.

Location: Scituate

Established: 1811

Tower height: 50 feet

Elevation of the focal plane: 70 feet

Optic: Modern

Status: Private aid to navigation

Characteristic: Flashes white every 15 seconds

Range: 10 miles

Position: 42° 12' 16
70° 42' 54

Note: Keeper's daughters held off a British warship in 1814

PLYMOUTH LIGHT

Location: Plymouth

Established: 1769

Tower height: 39 feet

Elevation of the focal plane: 102 feet

Optic: Modern (solar powered)

Status: Active

Characteristic: Flashes three times every 30 seconds (red sector)

Range: 17 miles

Position: 42° 00' 12 70° 36' 00

Note: America's first female keeper served here

One of the first navigational beacons in America, the original Plymouth Lighthouse was built in 1769 on the Gurnet, a long, narrow peninsula at the north end of Plymouth Bay. It displayed two beacons, one each from a pair of small, wooden towers perched on the roof of the keeper's house. The lights were not very effective at guiding mariners, but they did attract some unwanted attention from a British frigate that fired on the station during a Revolutionary War battle in 1778. The attack may have frightened local residents but not Hannah Thomas, who ignored the guns and kept the lights burning. Mrs. Thomas maintained the Plymouth Light from the time her husband died in 1776 until 1790, and she is generally recognized as America's first female lighthouse keeper.

In 1801 an accidental fire accomplished what the British had failed to do and destroyed the old lighthouse. Like the original, its replacement had two towers producing a double light that helped mariners distinguish the Plymouth beacon from others along the coast. Dry rot can do almost as much damage as fire, and by the 1840s the station's crumbling timbers forced the government to rebuild it once again. Completed in 1843, the new lighthouse had two octagonal, wooden towers, each of them equipped with an array of oil-burning lamps and reflectors. Later the towers were fitted with fourth-order Fresnel lenses.

During the 1920s the U.S. Lighthouse Service gave up on multiple light aids like the one here and converted them to single-light beacons. As a result the northeast tower at Plymouth Lighthouse was dismantled and hauled away. Now equipped with a modern optic, the remaining tower is still in use.

TO SEE THE LIGHT: Cruises taking visitors to within easy viewing distance of the lighthouse depart from piers along Water Street in Plymouth; call (800) 232–2469.

The Duxbury Pier Lighthouse rises like the head of a sea serpent from the waters of Plymouth Bay, where it has helped ships keep to the main channel since 1871. Located just off the end of an extensive pier, the station would be exposed to wind, waves, and high water, so it was built to resist the elements. Placed atop a massive caisson, its walls and lantern are of heavy, cast-iron construction. When seen from a distance, the structure suggests an enormous teakettle or coffeepot. As testament to its rugged, weather-resistant design, the lighthouse still stands and remains in operation more than 130 years after its completion.

TO SEE THE LIGHT: Although the lighthouse can be seen at a distance from the Plymouth waterfront, the best views are from the water. Cruises departing from piers along Water Street in Plymouth offer a closer look at this lighthouse as well as the historic Plymouth Lighthouse; call (800) 232–2469.

Location: Plymouth

Established: 1871

Tower height: 47 feet

Elevation of the focal plane: 35 feet

Optic: Modern (solar powered)

Status: Active

Characteristic: Two red flashes every 5 seconds

Range: 6 miles

Position: 41° 59' 12
70° 38' 54

Note: First coffeepot-style cast-iron lighthouse

Shirin Pagels

CHAPTER THREE:
PROVINCETOWN TO FALL RIVER

L ike a whirlpool of sand in the ocean, Cape Cod sweeps seaward from the far southeastern corner of Massachusetts, arching to the north and finally curling back on itself about 20 miles due east of Plymouth. Deposited by glaciers that blanketed New England during much of the last 100,000 years, the sands of the cape are constantly on the move, wearing away in one area and building up in another. Land has only a tenuous hold on this place, and the ocean seems always poised to rush in and reclaim the Cape as its own. But to mariners sailing westward out of the broad Atlantic, the high dunes of Cape Cod have always been a substantial and welcome sight. The Pilgrims first landed here in 1620, before sailing across Cape Cod Bay to step off onto Plymouth Rock. Once they had spotted the cape, the captains of clipper ships headed back from Europe, Africa, or China knew that Boston Harbor waited less than half a day's sail to the west. A sizable number of rugged New England whalers once called the Cape home, just as many fishermen do today.

However, if the Cape is a friend of sailors, it is also a threat. As a point of land extending far out into the Atlantic, the Cape is a formidable navigational obstacle that has ruined many good ships and killed many strong men. Four centuries of wrecks have filled the sands of its beaches with bits and pieces of vessels now long forgotten.

Cape Cod is just the sort of place where you would expect to find lighthouses, and, indeed, it boasts seven major lights. Most prominent is the Cape Cod Light, also known as the Highland Light. The tower stands on a high bluff near Truro, and its beacon, situated 183 feet above the sea, can be seen from a distance of nearly 24 miles. For sailors emerging from the dark reaches of the Atlantic, Cape Cod Light is often the first visual evidence that the North American continent is near.

Soon after the first Cape Cod tower was built in 1798, sailors began to confuse the light with the fixed beacon of the Boston Light, 41 miles to the northwest. To solve this problem, a rotating, opaque screen was placed in the lantern of the Cape Cod Light. Completing one revolution every eight minutes, the screen was supposed to make the light flash. But, as one grumbling mariner was quick to point out, the screen partially obscured the light much of the time and gave it "phases," like those of the moon. Such objections notwithstanding, the screen system was retained for many years. Cape Cod Light remains one of the most powerful in North America, although today it employs a dual electric beacon similar to those used at airports.

Henry David Thoreau made several visits to Cape Cod Light during the mid-1800s. Noting rapid erosion of the sandy cliff beneath the tower, Thoreau believed the lighthouse would soon fall from its precarious perch. Maritime officials apparently agreed and built a new tower some 500 feet from the precipice, far enough for it to resist erosion for another century and a half. The erosion continued, however, and during the 1990s, the venerable Cape Cod tower had to be moved to keep it from falling over the cliff.

Hundreds of ships have ended their days on Race Point, which forms Cape Cod's westward knuckle. Vessels must round the point to reach Provincetown Harbor a few miles to the southeast, and over the years more than a few have tried but failed. No one knows exactly how many ships have piled up on the sands of the point, but more than one hundred wrecks have been noted there since the establishment of the Race Point Light in 1816. No doubt countless others have been saved by the light's flashing white beacon, which can be seen from a distance of 16 miles.

Established in 1826 near the end of a sandy spit where the cape nearly completes a 360-degree inward spiral, Long Point Light still serves Provincetown Harbor with its flashing green light. During the Civil War authorities responded quickly to rumors of an impending attack by Confederate warships, building a pair of small earthen gun batteries near the lighthouse. The tiny Confederate Navy was never really up to such an expedition, however, and citizens of Provincetown soon dubbed the two batteries "Fort Harmless" and "Fort Useless."

About 15 miles southeast of Provincetown, the Nauset Beach Light helps guard the Cape's Atlantic shore. Established in 1838, this station originally displayed three lights shining from identical towers known to many locals as the "Three Sisters of Nauset." Eventually, the government determined that one light would serve just as well as three, whereupon two of the Nauset maidens suffered the indignity of being sold and converted for use as summer cottages. An iron tower was placed here in 1923 and still guides ships with alternating red and white flashes. The three old "Sisters" have been gathered into a small park not far from the lighthouse.

CAPE COD (HIGHLAND) LIGHT

A whorl of sparkling sand deposited by glaciers during the last ice age, Cape Cod is one of the world's most famous geological features. Extending far out into the stormy Atlantic from the southeastern corner of Massachusetts, the peninsula poses a formidable threat to seafaring vessels. Hence, Cape Cod became home to a remarkable array of lighthouses. The oldest and best known of these is the Cape Cod—also known as Highland—Lighthouse, established in 1798. Although its tower was only 30 feet high, the focal plane of its light, shining from atop a high, sandy bluff, was more than 150 feet above sea level. From this height whaling ships and schooners could see it from more than 20 miles out at sea.

Wind and water, the same forces that built the bluffs, also eat away at them and by the 1850s threatened to undercut the lighthouse and dump it into the sea. In 1857 a new 66-foot tower was built more than 500 feet from the nearest cliff. The erosion did not stop, however, and by the 1990s the cliffs were within 110 feet of the tower's foundation and coming closer every day. To save the lighthouse a committee of local preservationists raised $1.5 million to move it back a safe distance from the cliffs. Completed in 1997, the move was an extraordinary engineering feat accomplished in part by pushing the massive tower over rails lubricated with ordinary bath soap.

TO SEE THE LIGHT: From U.S. Highway 6 in Truro, follow the Cape Cod Light signs. Contact the Highland Museum and Lighthouse, P.O. Box 486, Truro, MA 02666 for more information; or call (508) 487–1121.

Location: Truro

Established: 1798

Tower height: 66 feet

Elevation of the focal plane: 183 feet

Optic: Modern

Status: Active

Characteristic: Flashes white every 5 seconds

Range: 18 miles

Position: 42° 02' 22
70° 03' 39

Note: Pushed back from the cliff's edge on rails

RACE POINT LIGHT

N o one is sure how many ships have ended their days on Race Point, which forms a sandy knuckle at the far northern tip of Cape Cod. Vessels must round the point to enter Cape Cod Bay or to reach the safety of Provincetown on the Cape's protected inner shore. Over the years more than a few have failed to reach their destination. In 1816 U.S. maritime officials ordered construction of a lighthouse to make navigating the swirling waters off Race Point a little easier.

Completed in 1816, the station was given a 25-foot stone tower and a modest dwelling enabling the keeper and his family to maintain a wholesome, if rustic, existence. Although only a few miles from the bustle of Provincetown, this bucolic light station was surrounded by acres of trackless, shifting sand and might as well have been on a desert island. Over the years the keeper's residence was enlarged and upgraded, but the station itself remained no less remote.

In 1876 the original stone structure was replaced by a forty-five-foot-tall, cast-iron tower.

Otherwise, little changed here until 1978 when the Coast Guard automated the Race Point Light and removed the station's last keepers. Afterward, the abandoned wood-frame residence fell into disrepair and might have been demolished save for the efforts of a preservationist group called the New England Lighthouse Foundation—known today as the American Lighthouse Foundation, the nation's foremost champion of lighthouse preservation. Painstakingly restored, the old home is usually open to visitors during the summer and is available for overnight stays.

TO SEE THE LIGHT: From U.S. Highway 6 in Provincetown, take Race Point Road to Race Point Beach. Two miles of soft sand separate the parking area from the lighthouse, and the hike is recommended only for veteran walkers—be sure to wear old shoes. For more information on the station or on overnight accommodations, call (781) 740–4290.

Location: Near Provincetown

Established: 1816

Tower height: 45 feet

Elevation of the focal plane: 41 feet

Optic: Modern (solar powered)

Status: Active

Characteristic: Flashes white every 10 seconds

Range: 16 miles

Position: 42° 03' 45
70° 14' 35

Note: Guards the far northwestern shore of Cape Cod

Shirin Pagels

📫 📷

Location: Near Provincetown

Established: 1873

Tower height: 39 feet

Elevation of the focal plane: 45 feet

Optic: Modern (solar powered)

Status: Active

Characteristic: Flashes red every 10 seconds

Range: 13 miles

Position: 42° 01' 16 70° 11' 37

Note: One of three active lights that serve Provincetown

In 1872, a 39-foot light tower was erected on the rolling dunes at Wood End to help guide ships into Provincetown Harbor. The structure was not very different from the one built at about that same time on Long Point near the end of the Cape Cod arm. Both structures still stand and continue to serve mariners. However, the Wood End dwelling and storage shed were razed when the station was automated during the 1960s.

Like the lighthouses at Race Point and Long Point, the squared-off tower at Wood End stands atop coarse sands, which were dumped into the Atlantic by glaciers long ago and washed onto the shores of Cape Cod by the tides. In fact, the Cape is made up almost entirely of this glacial material. In some places, such as a long bluff facing the open Atlantic, the sands crumble and are carried away by the current. In others, as near, Provincetown, they are deposited once again in the form of long beaches and sand flats.

TO SEE THE LIGHT: A breakwater beginning at the end of Commercial Street in Provincetown leads to the Wood End Light Station, but the walk is strenuous and should not be attempted in rough weather.

LONG POINT LIGHT

Since 1826 the Long Point Light has guided mariners to Provincetown. It shines from a tower at the very end of Cape Cod, the tip of a sandy arm reaching back toward the east and forming a natural breakwater for the harbor. The original lighthouse consisted of a modest residence with a small tower and lantern rising from its roof.

In time a thriving fishing village grew up around the lighthouse, and during the Civil War a pair of forts were built on the point to protect against Confederate raids. The gray raiders never came, and the village outlived the war by only a few years. Many of the houses that once stood there were floated across the harbor to Provincetown where some still stand. By 1876 the lighthouse itself was torn down and replaced by the existing brick structure. The Coast Guard automated the station and removed the keepers in 1952.

TO SEE THE LIGHT: Long Point Light is all but impossible to reach from land, but a water shuttle based in Provincetown provides access; call (508) 487–0898 or (800) 750–0898. A distant view of the station can be had from MacMillan Wharf in Provincetown.

Location: Near Provincetown

Established: 1826

Tower height: 38 feet

Elevation of the focal plane: 36 feet

Optic: Modern (solar powered)

Status: Active

Characteristic: Green occulting every 4 seconds

Range: 8 miles

Position: 42° 02' 00 70° 09' 42

Note: Located on the inward tip of Cape Cod

THREE SISTERS LIGHTHOUSES

ape Cod was once overcrowded with navigational lights. To help mariners tell one light from another, maritime officials gave each beacon a distinct appearance or characteristic: fixed, flashing, white, red, green, etc. In some cases lighthouses made their signals distinct by displaying two or, in rare instances, three separate lights. For more than seventy years, just such a three-light maritime beacon shined from the high, sandy bluffs above Nauset Beach.

Established in 1838, the light station that came to be called the "Three Sisters of Nauset" consisted of three small towers spaced a short distance apart at the top of the sea cliffs not far from the town of Eastham. Only 15 feet tall, the original brick towers were the work of Winslow Lewis, a government contractor who built dozens of early nineteenth-century lighthouses, equipping them with a mostly ineffective lamp-and-lens optic of his own design. Like his optics, Lewis's Nauset towers were of poor quality, but somehow they stood until 1892 when, undercut by erosion, they toppled over the cliffs. They were soon replaced by three lightweight iron towers that could be easily moved if threatened by erosion.

In the end the Nauset Sisters were undone neither by shoddy workmanship nor by nature, but by progress. By the early twentieth century, improvements in navigational technology had made multiple-light beacons obsolete, and the Lighthouse Service decided to stop using them. In 1911 Nauset was converted to a single-light station, and two of its towers were sold off to local landowners for $3.50 each. A few years later, the remaining Sister was replaced by a larger and more substantial tower moved here from nearby Chatham.

Location: Eastham

Established: 1838

Tower height: 29 feet

Elevation of the focal plane: 95 feet

Status: Deactivated in 1911

Note: Rare three-light maritime beacon

During the 1970s the National Park Service bought the old towers from various private owners and moved them to a small park not far from the existing Nauset Beach Lighthouse. The reunited Sisters now serve as an attraction of the Cape Cod National Seashore.

TO SEE THE LIGHTS: From Route 6 in Eastham, follow the signs to Nauset Light Beach. The Three Sisters are arrayed in a small, forested park not far from the current Nauset Beach Light. For more information on the Cape Cod National Seashore, call (508) 255–3421.

NAUSET BEACH LIGHT

Location: Eastham

Established: 1838

Tower height: 48 feet

Elevation of the focal
plane: 114 feet

Optic: Modern
(solar powered)

Status: Active

Characteristic: Alternating
white and red every
5 seconds

Range: 24 miles

Position: 41° 51' 36
69° 57' 12

Note: Iron tower from
Chatham replaced the
"Three Sisters"

A line a high, sandy cliffs form a more-or-less continuous wall along the Atlantic shores of Cape Cod. The wall is not made of strong stuff, however, and has been crumbling away ever since fishermen and whalers first settled here hundreds of years ago. Not surprisingly, the wall is guarded by a number of maritime beacons: in the north by the famous Highland Light (also known as the Cape Cod Lighthouse), in the south by the Chatham Light, and in between, about halfway along the Cape's outer arm, by the Nauset Beach Light.

Established in 1838, the beacon above Nauset Beach originally consisted of three lights rather than just one. The unusual triple light of the Three Sisters of Nauset was readily distinguishable from other beacons to the north and south. The lights also made it easier for mariners to sail parallel to the coast by keeping the lights off either the port or starboard side of the ship. Eventually, the government determined that one light would serve just as well as three, whereupon two of Nauset's maidens were sold to private owners for a pittance—just $3.50 each. In 1923 the 48-foot, cast-iron tower that stands there today was brought to Nauset from Chatham, where it had been part of a twin-towered, two-light system since 1877.

In time the steadily eroding cliffs threatened to undercut the tower and pitch it onto the beach below. As with most other lighthouses threatened by erosion, this one could only be saved by relocating it. In 1996 the ninety-ton structure was moved to a safer

location several hundred feet from the cliffs. Now owned by the
National Park Service, Nauset Beach Light remains in operation,
warning mariners with a flashing red and white light.

TO SEE THE LIGHT: From Route 6 in Eastham, follow Brackett
Road, Nauset Road, Cable Road, and then Ocean View Drive to the
Nauset Beach Lighthouse parking area. The partially restored Three
Sisters towers are in a small, nearby park.

CHATHAM LIGHT

Location: Chatham

Established: 1808

Tower height: 48 feet

Elevation of the focal
plane: 80 feet

Optic: Modern

Status: Active

Characteristic: Flashes
twice every 10 seconds

Range: 24 miles

Position: 41° 40' 17
69° 57' 01

Note: Previously displayed
two lights

The large number of navigational beacons beaming seaward from Cape Cod tended to confuse mariners, and maritime officials struggled to give each light a distinctive appearance. After 1808 a matched pair of octagonal, wooden towers at Chatham marked the town's busy harbor with a rare double light. It predated by several decades an even more unusual triple beacon—the Three Sisters—established at Nauset Beach in 1838.

The Chatham Lights anchored the southern end of a line of sea cliffs stretching along the Atlantic shore of the Cape's outer arm. The cliffs are highly unstable, and erosion eventually threatens any structure built on top of them. The twin Chatham sentinels served for little more thirty years before the eroding cliffs forced the government to pull them down and erect new brick towers at what seemed a safe distance from the edge. Nothing could stop the westward march of the cliffs, however, and in 1879 the south tower fell over them and ended up in a heap on the beach. Two years later the north tower and keeper's house followed the south tower over the hungry precipice. Fortunately, by that time, the government had built yet another lighthouse complete with matching 48-foot towers constructed of cast-iron so they could be moved, if necessary.

Although the new station never had to be relocated, one of its iron towers eventually ended up elsewhere. During the early 1920s, the U.S. Lighthouse Service discontinued all its multiple-light signals, and Chatham became a single-light beacon. Rendered obsolete by the change, one of the Chatham towers, the Nauset Beach Light, was moved about 15 miles north to Eastham, where it replaced the famed Three Sisters of Nauset.

TO SEE THE LIGHT: Chatham's Main Street leads directly to the lighthouse. Although the station is not open to the public, the view from the street is excellent.

Nobska's historic keeper's dwelling was covered with natural-color wood shingles after this photo was taken.

NOBSKA POINT LIGHT

A few miles from Woods Hole, at the far southwestern end of Cape Cod, a pair of vicious shoals lurk beneath the waters of Vineyard Sound. Known locally as the Hedge Fence and L'Hommedieu, these submerged dragons have claimed more than their share of vessels large and small. But since 1829, the Nobska Point Light has warned mariners to keep their distance and, so, made passing through the sound a little safer.

The first lighthouse built here was a simple stone cottage with a lantern on top. Weather and time took a heavy toll on the station, and by the 1870s it was literally falling apart. In 1876 the Lighthouse Board replaced the old Nobska tower with a prefabricated cast-iron cylinder, which was built in a shipyard and brought to Woods Holes in four sections. Once the pieces were bolted together, the iron shell was lined with brick and fitted with a fourth-order Fresnel lens.

Together with its classical lens, the light still guards the shoals and guides tourist-laden ferries across the sound from Martha's Vineyard. Sailors near the shoals see a red beacon, whereas those in safe water see a white one.

TO SEE THE LIGHT: Located off Nobska Road in Woods Hole, the lighthouse grounds are open to the public every day until dark. On occasion the tower is open as well. A fine view of the light can be had from the Martha's Vineyard Ferry. For schedules and reservations call the Steamship Authority at (508) 477–8600 or (508) 693–9130.

Location: Woods Hole

Established: 1829

Tower height: 40 feet

Elevation of the focal plane: 87 feet

Optic: Fresnel lens (fourth order)

Status: Active

Characteristic: Flashes white every 6 seconds (red sector)

Range: 13 miles

Position: 41° 30' 57
70° 39' 18

Note: Brick-lined iron tower

HYANNIS HARBOR LIGHTHOUSE

For many years travelers or Hyannis locals might have passed this old tower and never imagined it had once been a lighthouse. Decommissioned in 1929 after eighty years of service, the building was sold to owners who lopped off the lantern and used the remaining structure as part of a private residence. In 1985 the home was purchased by an antique dealer who valued the tower's history and replaced its lantern.

TO SEE THE LIGHT: Still part of a residence, the Hyannis Harbor tower is on private property and closed to the public. It can be seen from the end of Harbor Road in South Hyannis or from the water.

Location: Hyannis

Established: 1849

Tower height: 19 feet

Elevation of the focal plane: 42 feet

Status: Deactivated in 1929

Note: Now part of a private residence

BUTLER FLATS LIGHT

Shirin Pagels

Location: New Bedford

Established: 1898

Tower height: 53 feet

Elevation of the focal
plane: 53 feet

Optic: Modern
(solar powered)

Status: Active

Characteristic: Flashes
white every 4 seconds

Range: 4 miles

Position: 41° 36' 12
70° 53' 42

Note: Caisson-style tower
sometimes called a
"sparkplug light"

Built in open water atop a concrete-filled cast-iron caisson, the Butler Flats Lighthouse marks the main channel used by vessels approaching New Bedford. Completed in 1898, the station has a brick, rather than cast-iron, tower, a fact that sets it apart from other so-called "sparkplug" lighthouses.

So called because of their distinctive appearance, sparkplug lighthouses are, for the same reason, sometimes called "teakettle" or "coffeepot" lights. The massive caissons that serve as the foundations for these lights help protect them from high water and ice. Open-water lighthouses were once built on pilings rather than caissons, but these structures proved much too vulnerable to foul weather and ice floes.

TO SEE THE LIGHT: The lighthouse can be seen from the New Bedford waterfront or from the New Bedford–to–Martha's Vineyard ferry. For ferry information call (508) 997–1688.

CLARK'S POINT LIGHT

Intended to guide vessels to New Bedford, the original Clark's Point Lighthouse served for more than sixty years before relinquishing its view of the water to a great stone fort. Begun during the Civil War, Fort Taber (later known as Fort Rodman) eventually blocked the tower's beacon with its massive walls. Consequently, maritime authorities ordered the lantern room removed from the 42-foot stone tower and placed on the walls of the fort. This makeshift arrangement worked well enough, and the Clark's Point Light remained in operation until 1898, when the nearby Butler Flats Lighthouse was completed. After a century of disuse, the fortress lighthouse was restored by the City of New Bedford. In 2001 it was reopened and now serves as both an active maritime light and a historical monument.

TO SEE THE LIGHT: From Route 18 in New Bedford, take the downtown exit and follow Water Street, Cove Road, and then east Rodney French Boulevard to the Fort Rodman parking lot. The lighthouse rises from the inner walls of the fort. It also can be seen from the New Bedford–to–Martha's Vineyard ferry. For ferry information call (508) 997–1688.

Location: New Bedford

Established: 1804

Tower height: 42 feet

Elevation of the focal plane: 68 feet

Optic: Modern

Status: Private aid to navigation

Characteristic: Flashes every 4 seconds

Range: 9 miles

Position: 41° 35' 32
70° 54' 02

Note: Relit in 2001 after a century of disuse

Shirin Pagels

PALMER'S ISLAND LIGHT

📷

Location New Bedford

Established: 1849

Tower height: 42 feet

Elevation of the focal plane: 24 feet

Optic: Modern (solar powered)

Status: Private aid to navigation

Characteristic: Flashes white every 4 seconds

Range: 5 miles

Position: 41° 47' 36
70° 54' 36

Note: Reactivated in 1999 after many years of disuse

The Palmer's Island Lighthouse was built in 1849 to mark the entrance to New Bedford Harbor, at that time home of the nation's largest whaling fleet. More than 200 vessels depended on its light to see them and their cargoes of valuable whale oil safely into port. With the introduction of cheap fuels such as kerosene and the depletion of whale populations around the world, the New Bedford whaling fleet declined and eventually disappeared altogether. Even so, Palmer's Island Light remained vital to mariners and continued in operation for more than a century.

In late September 1938 a mighty hurricane swept over lower New England, driving a wall of water into the harbor and killing Mabel Small, the wife of keeper Arthur Small. Hurricane damage further diminished the importance of the port and its beacon, and Palmer's Island Lighthouse was eventually abandoned.

After the Coast Guard snuffed out its light in 1963, the tower fell into disrepair. In 1966 vandals set fire to the tower, leaving it a gutted ruin. Fortunately, the building was not torn down, and during the 1970s it was partially restored. A second restoration in 1999 returned the structure to its former glory, and its beacon was relit as a private aid to navigation. Generally speaking, private aids like this one are not needed for navigation, but are maintained for aesthetic of historical purposes. Even so, mariners may still occasionally use them to find a safe channel into harbor.

TO SEE THE LIGHT: Palmer's Island and its lighthouse can be reached only at low tide via the New Bedford hurricane barrier. The tower can also be seen from the Cuttyhunk Island Ferry; call (508) 992–1432. While in the area be sure to visit the New Bedford Whaling Museum on Johnny Cake Hill; call (508) 997–0046.

Shirin Pagels

Shirin Pagels

Set atop a massive open-water caisson, Borden Flats Light points the way to Fall River, known to many as the home of Lizzie Borden, the famous New England spinster who was accused of murdering her parents with an ax. Although Lizzie was acquitted of the crime, her story continues to fascinate murder-mystery fans. Far less famous is the cast-iron, sparkplug–style Borden Flats Lighthouse (said to be named for Lizzie's family), which dates from 1881. Severely damaged by a hurricane in 1938, the lighthouse was restored and remains in operation to this day.

The same mighty storm that blasted the Borden Flats tower in 1938 also mauled light stations and waterfront properties all along the coast of southern New England. The storm scored a direct hit on Rhode Island's Narragansett Bay and, striking at high tide, flooded entire towns and villages. Fall River, Massachusetts, at the far northeastern corner of the bay, suffered severe damage, as did its lighthouse.

TO SEE THE LIGHT: In Fall River drive southeast along Broadway, turn right on Bradford Avenue, then right again on Almond Street. The lighthouse can be seen from the Borden Flat Marina off Almond.

Location: Fall River

Established: 1881

Tower height: 50 feet

Elevation of the focal plane: 47 feet

Optic: Modern

Status: Active

Characteristic: Flashes white every 2.5 seconds

Range: 11 miles

Position: 41° 42' 18
71° 10' 30

Note: Said to be named for the family of Lizzie Borden

CHAPTER FOUR:
NANTUCKET AND MARTHA'S VINEYARD

N o Massachusetts lighthouse adventure would be complete without a visit to the famous islands of Martha's Vineyard and Nantucket. Settled hundreds of years ago by whalers and fishermen, the islands are rich in history and maritime tradition. Naturally, they are also ringed by lighthouses, most still in operation. Nantucket has three shining navigational beacons, while Martha's Vineyard can claim no fewer than five.

Although both islands have airports, most travelers reach them by way of ferries embarking from Hyannis, Falmouth, or Woods Hole—all on Cape Cod. Ferries approaching Nantucket are guided into port by the white flashing Great Point Light or the red beacon on Brant Point near the harbor entrance. Lighthouse beacons are romantic, especially when seen from offshore, and to view these historic lights from the waters of Nantucket Sound must be counted among the chief attractions of any island visit.

Of course these lighthouses were not built for emotional or romantic reasons. Originally, their purpose was entirely practical. Nantucket Island whalers and merchant seamen wanted to get their vessels in and out of port without running aground on rocks and shallows, so in 1746 they turned to their community for help. Their plea resulted in the construction of a modest light tower on Brant Point. After the Boston Light (built in 1716), this beacon is the second oldest in the United States, although the tower seen today is little more than a century old. Built in 1901, it is the latest of as many as ten different light towers that have stood here. Earlier towers here fell victim to calamity or dry rot at a rate of about one every fifteen years over a period of more than one and a half centuries.

The Great Point Light on Nantucket's far northeastern tip has been far less exasperating to the local citizenry. Built in 1784, it burned down only once, in 1816. Better still, from the point of view of the islanders, the original tower was paid for by the Commonwealth of Massachusetts, and its replacement, completed in 1816, by the U.S. government. Built of stone, the 1816 tower stood just over 70 feet tall and served the island faithfully for nearly 179 years. Unfortunately, the old lighthouse finally yielded to nature. Knocked down by a gale during the 1980s, it has been replaced by a nearly exact replica.

Although not a likely victim of storm, Nantucket's third lighthouse, located on Sankaty Head, is highly vulnerable to erosion. Like the historic Highland and Nauset Beach towers on Cape Cod, it stands atop a line of crumbling sea cliffs that are steadily retreating westward. Steps have been taken to reduce the erosion, but they will not long succeed. Unless the tower is moved—and soon—it will be lost forever.

At least as rich in maritime history as Nantucket, Martha's Vineyard has even more lighthouses—five in all, and each of them still functions. As with Nantucket, "The Vineyard" receives most of her visitors via ferry. Usually, the first light ferry passengers see as they approach the island is that of the West Chop Lighthouse near Vineyard Haven. An occulting beacon, the light winks at them once every four seconds.

Since it remains an active Coast Guard facility, the West Chop Station is not open to the public, but you can get close enough to take a good photograph.

Other Martha's Vineyard lighthouses are more visitor friendly. The most histori-cally significant of them is the two-century-old Gay Head Lighthouse, which guards a line of brightly colored cliffs at the far western end of the island.

Probably the best known of the island beacons is the Edgartown Lighthouse. Visitors can stroll about its grounds to their heart's content, and the Martha's Vineyard Historical Society occasionally opens the all-cast-iron tower for tours. The society maintains an impressive Edgartown museum complex with a separate building to house the giant first-order Fresnel lens that once served at Gay Head.

The other light stations on Martha's Vineyard are less easy to reach, but if you try hard enough, you can get to them, and it's certainly worth the effort. If you should manage to see all five of the Vineyard lights in a single weekend, you should celebrate with a fine lobster dinner. And if you should fail? Well, then, celebrate anyway, and bon appétit!

The historic Gay Head Lighthouse marks the western end of Martha's Vineyard.

Shirin Pagels

BRANT POINT LIGHT

Location: Nantucket

Established: 1746

Tower height: 28 feet

Elevation of the focal
plane: 26 feet

Optic: Modern
(solar powered)

Status: Active

Characteristic: Red
occulting every 4 seconds

Range: 10 miles

Position: 41° 17' 24
70° 05' 25

Note: America's second
oldest light station

Nothing is more democratic than a New England town meeting. If a town is to part with so much as a dime, then a majority of the community must agree on spending it. And since no one wants to appear loose with their neighbors' money, the budgets that emerge from such meetings are notoriously tightfisted. So it is ironic that North America's second-oldest light station owes its existence to a town meeting held on Nantucket Island in 1746. On January 24th of that year, the sea captains of the island addressed their fellow citizens and asked for money to build a lighthouse. In a rare fit of fiscal openhandedness, the people of Nantucket offered to raise 200 pounds sterling for the project, and not long afterward a little wooden lighthouse was built on Brant Point at the entrance to Nantucket Harbor. At the time only one other lighthouse stood in all of Britain's North American colonies: the stone tower on Boston's Little Brewster Island.

Unfortunately, the Brant Point Light would not have as distinguished a career as its larger neighbor to the north. It burned to the ground only a dozen years after its construction. At another town meeting held the following year, citizens once again opened their purses, and money was raised for another tower. This one was knocked down by a windstorm in 1774. The *Massachusetts Gazette* reported: "We hear from Nantucket that on Wednesday the 9th of March, Instant at about 8 o'clock, they had a most violent Gust of Wind that perhaps was ever known there, but it lasted only a minute. It seemed to come in a narrow Vein, and in its progress blew down and totally destroyed the Light-House on that Island besides several Shops, Barns, etc." The citizens of Nantucket then paid for yet another tower, which burned down in 1783. At this point the islanders may have felt they were throwing good money after bad, and indeed, later Brant Point towers were to prove disastrously vulnerable to wind, fire, and rot. In all, ten different lighthouses have stood on Brant Point.

By far the most durable of them has been the existing lighthouse, which has marked the point since 1901. Its white, cylindrical wooden tower raises its lantern only 26 feet above the water, making it the lowest light in New England. Its red light can be seen from about 10 miles away.

TO SEE THE LIGHT: For ferries serving Nantucket Island, call the Steamship Authority at (508) 477–8600 or (508) 693–9139. The lighthouse is within walking distance of the ferry terminal. While on the island, don't miss the Nantucket Whaling Museum; call (508) 228–1894.

SANKATY HEAD LIGHT

Standing atop a line of soaring sea cliffs, the 70-foot brick tower of Sankaty Head Lighthouse dominates Nantucket's southeastern shore. Built in 1850, the tower was fitted with a Fresnel lens, the first in Massachusetts. For years this large second-order lens was rotated by a clockwork mechanism driven by weights suspended on cables. The keeper had to climb the tower frequently to "rewind" the device. In 1950 the station's historic lens was replaced by a smaller modern optic. The original lens was given to the Nantucket Whaling Museum, where it remains on display.

Like a number of other historic lighthouses in Massachusetts and elsewhere, this one is seriously threatened by erosion. Unless something is done to save it, the old tower will eventually topple over the Nantucket cliffs.

TO SEE THE LIGHT: For ferries serving Nantucket Island, call the Steamship Authority at (508) 477–8600 or (508) 693–9139. The light station is located off Baxter Road on the east side of the island. To see the old Sankaty Head Fresnel lens, visit the Nantucket Whaling Museum; call (508) 228–1894.

Location: Nantucket

Established: 1850

Tower height: 70 feet

Elevation of the focal plane: 158 feet

Optic: Modern

Status: Active

Characteristic: Flashes white every 7.5 seconds

Range: 24 miles

Position: 41° 17' 01
69° 57' 54

Note: Among New England's most powerful seacoast lights

Courtesy U.S. Coast Guard

S ome Atlantic storms are so powerful that nothing can stand in their way, not even tall, stone lighthouses. In March 1984 a gale swept over Nantucket, and when it had passed, the 60-foot stone tower that had marked Great Point since 1816 lay in a heap on the sand. Unhappy with the loss of so historic a structure, Nantucket residents pressured Congress, and a replica of the fallen lighthouse was built two years later not far from its original site.

The new lighthouse serves the same purpose as the old one: guarding the long arm of land extending several miles northward from the east side of the island. The light helps vessels inbound from the Atlantic avoid the point and swing around into Nantucket Harbor. A wooden lighthouse marked Great Point as early as 1784.

TO SEE THE LIGHT: The Great Point Lighthouse is located at the far northeastern end of Nantucket Island on a long spit of land, most of which is included in the Coskata-Coatue Wildlife Refuge. For tours of the refuge and lighthouse property, call (508) 228–6799 or (508) 228–1951. For ferries serving Nantucket Island, call the Steamship Authority at (508) 477–8600 or (508) 693–9139.

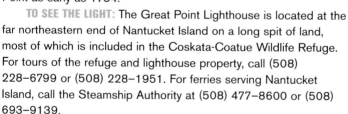

Location: Nantucket

Established: 1784

Tower height: 60 feet

Elevation of the focal plane: 71 feet

Optic: Modern (solar powered)

Status: Active

Characteristic: Flashes white every 5 seconds (red sector)

Range: 14 miles

Position: 41° 23' 25
70° 02' 54

Note: Original tower destroyed in a 1984 storm

EDGARTOWN HARBOR LIGHT

Shirin Pagels

Location: Martha's Vineyard

Established: 1828

Tower height: 45 feet

Elevation of the focal plane: 45 feet

Optic: Modern (solar powered)

Status: Active

Characteristic: Flashes every 4 seconds

Range: 5 miles

Position: 41° 23' 27
70° 30' 11

Note: Iron tower brought by barge from northern Massachusetts

The cast-iron tower that now marks Edgartown Harbor on Martha's Vineyard was built in 1875 and originally stood at Ipswich, well to the north of Boston. In 1939 it was pulled down, loaded onto a barge, and shipped to Edgartown. The relocated tower replaced the station's historic 1828 Cape Cod–style lighthouse, which had been destroyed by a hurricane. For many years a fourth-order Fresnel lens served this station and mariners who depended on its beacon to guide them to Edgartown. The classic lens was removed in 1988 and replaced by a modern optic.

The Edgartown Harbor Lighthouse is managed by the Martha's Vineyard Historical Society. In addition to this and other lighthouses on the island, the society maintains several historic buildings in Edgartown as well as a museum and a specially built display tower containing the first-order Fresnel lens that once served at Gay Head.

TO SEE THE LIGHT: The lighthouse can be reached via Main Street and Water Street in Edgartown. The Martha's Vineyard Historical Society offers occasional tours; call (508) 627–4441. For ferries serving Martha's Vineyard, call the Steamship Authority at (508) 477–8600 or (508) 693–9139.

CAPE POGE LIGHT

Two years after the Gay Head Light (1799) began to shine and guide ships around the western end of Martha's Vineyard, the government established a light at Cape Poge about 20 miles to the east. Completed for a bargain basement price of $2,000, the Cape Poge tower was a modest wooden building protected from the weather by shingles. Lifting its light about 35 feet above the island sands, it stood until 1838 when it was replaced by a similar wooden structure.

This second Cape Poge Lighthouse lasted only six years, and the station received a third tower in 1844, a fourth in 1880, and yet another in 1893. The latter lighthouse still stands but not on its original site. Erosion forced relocations in 1907, 1922, 1960, and 1987.

TO SEE THE LIGHT: Chappaquiddick Island can be reached via a five-minute ferry ride from Edgartown (call the Steamship Authority at 508–477–8600 or 508–693–9139), but getting to the lighthouse may be a little more difficult. Once on the island follow Chappaquiddick Road and Dike Road to Dike Bridge. From the bridge you have to hike 3.5 miles over soft sand to reach the lighthouse. For tours call (508) 627–3599.

Location: Chappaquiddick Island, Martha's Vineyard

Established: 1801

Tower height: 35 feet

Elevation of the focal plane: 65 feet

Optic: Modern (solar powered)

Status: Active

Characteristic: Flashes white every 6 seconds

Range: 9 miles

Position: 41° 25' 10 70° 27' 08

Note: Tower has been rebuilt or moved repeatedly

Shirin Pagels

GAY HEAD LIGHT

Of the several navigational stations on Martha's Vineyard, the oldest and most impressive is the Gay Head Light. The headland takes its name from the bright colors streaking its cliffs. The tower, built atop the cliffs in 1799, took advantage of the cliffs' considerable height to raise its lantern far above the sea. The original Gay Head Lighthouse had an eight-sided wooden tower rising about 50 feet above the cliffs. The Lighthouse Board ordered construction of a new tower in 1856, and this time the builder used brick. A first-order Fresnel lens once focused the light, but it has been replaced by a more easily maintained modern optic.

TO SEE THE LIGHT: Located on the far western point of Martha's Vineyard, Gay Head Light can be reached by road from either North Haven or Edgartown. For ferries serving Martha's Vineyard, call the Steamship Authority at (508) 477–8600 or (508) 693–9139. The Martha's Vineyard Historical Society maintains a complex of historic buildings and exhibits including the old first-order Fresnel lens from Gay Head. The complex is located in Edgartown on School Street about two blocks southwest of Main; call (508) 627–4441.

Location: Martha's Vineyard

Established: 1799

Tower height: 51 feet

Elevation of the focal plane: 170 feet

Optic: Modern

Status: Active

Characteristic: Flashing white and red at 15-second intervals

Range: 24 miles

Position: 41° 20' 54 70° 50' 06

Note: Stands atop colorful cliffs

Shirin Pagels

WEST CHOP LIGHT

Location: Martha's Vineyard

Established: 1818

Tower height: 45 feet

Elevation of the focal plane: 84 feet

Optic: Fresnel lens (fourth order)

Status: Active

Characteristic: Occulting every 4 seconds (red sector)

Range: 14 miles

Position: 41° 28' 51 70° 35' 59

Note: Marks the entrance to Vineyard Haven Harbor

Vineyard Haven, once known as Holmes Hole, was the busiest port on the island during the early nineteenth century. Local mariners had to petition the government several times before Congress finally coughed up the money for a lighthouse in 1817. Completed the following year, the station cost $4,900 and consisted of a stone tower and a pair of two-story residences for keepers. The existing 45-foot brick tower dates to 1891. The station residences date to 1847, but were renovated during the 1890s in a distinctly Victorian style. Since it serves primarily as a harbor light, the West Chop beacon is focused by a relatively modest fourth-order Fresnel lens. Although only a fraction the size of the giant first-order lens that once served at Gay Head—and now on display in Edgartown— the West Chop lens produces a light visible from 14 miles away.

TO SEE THE LIGHT: Although not open to the public, West Chop Light can be seen from ferries approaching Martha's Vineyard or from West Chop Road off Main Street in Vineyard Haven. The lighthouse is located in a small municipal park in Oak Bluffs. For additional information on ferries, call the Steamship Authority at (508) 477–8600 or (508) 693–9139.

Shirin Pagels

Shirin Pagels

N o doubt frustrated by the lack of a government light signal on
the east side of Vineyard Haven Harbor, a Martha's Vineyard
shipmaster named Silas Daggett took matters into his own
hands. Soliciting donations from local merchants and seamen, he
built a modest light tower on Telegraph Hill in 1869. It soon burned
down and was replaced by a makeshift light on top of a house.

In 1878 federal maritime officials finally took Daggett's hint and
established an official light station at East Chop. The 40-foot cast-
iron tower assembled here at that time still stands and continues to
serve mariners. Although painted white now, the tower was once a
dark brown color, earning it the nickname "Chocolate Lighthouse."

TO SEE THE LIGHT: The lighthouse is located in a small municipal
park in Oak Bluffs. It can be seen from ferries crossing back and forth
between Martha's Vineyard and the mainland. For additional information on ferries, call the Steamship Authority at (508) 477–8600 or
(508) 693–9139.

Location: Martha's
Vineyard

Established: 1869

Tower height: 40 feet

Elevation of the focal
plane: 70 feet

Optic: Modern

Status: Active

Characteristic: Flashes
green every 6 seconds

Range: 9 miles

Position: 41° 28' 13
70° 34' 03

Note: "Chocolate
Lighthouse" built by a
local seaman

GLOSSARY

Argand lamp

A clean-burning oil lamp widely used in lighthouses during the late eighteenth and early nineteenth centuries. Designed by French inventor Francois-Pierre-Ami Argand, they produced an intense flame and a very bright light.

Automated light

A lighthouse with no keeper. Following World War II, remote-control systems, light-activated switches, and fog-sensing devices made automation an increasingly cost-effective and attractive option, and the efficiency-minded Coast Guard automated one light station after another. By 1970 only about sixty lighthouses had full-time keepers, and within two decades all but one of those beacons had been automated. Appropriately enough, historic Boston Light, automated in 1998, was the last to give up its keeper.

Beacon

A light or radio signal intended to guide mariners or aviators.

Bug light

From a distance lighthouses built on piles in open water look a bit like water bugs floating on the surface, hence the nickname "bug light." However, some old-time mariners claim bug lights got their name from the enormous number of insects attracted by their beacons. Perhaps the best known bug light was Boston's Narrows Light, built in 1856 and destroyed by fire in 1929.

Caisson towers

During the late nineteenth century, the government began building offshore lighthouses on caissons. A caisson is a hollow shell made of heavy, rolled-iron plates. Bolted together on land, the caisson was hauled to the construction site, sunk into the seabed up to a depth of about 30 feet, and then filled with sand, gravel, rock, or concrete. Completed in 1871, Duxbury Pier Light near Plymouth is said to be the oldest caisson tower in the United States.

Cast-iron towers

Introduced as a building material during the 1840s, cast iron revolutionized lighthouse construction. Stronger than stone and relatively light, cast iron made it possible to fabricate parts of a light tower in a far-off foundry and then ship them to the construction site for assembly. A cylindrical structure assembled in 1844 on Long Island Head in Boston Harbor may have been the first all–cast-iron lighthouse.

Characteristic

The identifying feature of a lighthouse beacon. To help mariners distinguish one beacon from another, maritime officials give each light in a given region a distinct color or pattern of flashes. Among the more famous lighthouse characteristics is that of the offshore Minots Ledge Lighthouse near Scituate, Massachusetts, which displays a single flash, follow by four quick flashes, then three more. This one-four-three flashing sequence reminds some romantic observers of I-LOVE-YOU.

Coast Guard

Since 1939 lighthouses and other aids to navigation in the United States have been the responsibility of the U.S. Coast Guard. Previously, the nation's maritime lights were maintained by a separate government agency known as the U.S. Lighthouse Service.

Colonial lighthouses

Before the American Revolution, only eleven lighthouses were built along the coast of what would later become the United States. These colonial lights are listed here by year of construction. Boston Harbor Lighthouse (1716 in Massachusetts); Tybee Island Lighthouse (1742 in Georgia); Brant Point Lighthouse (1746 in Massachusetts); Beavertail Lighthouse (1749 in Rhode Island); New London Harbor Lighthouse (1760 in Connecticut); Sandy Hook Lighthouse (1764 in New Jersey); Cape Henlopen Lighthouse (1767 in Delaware); Morris Island Lighthouse (1767 in South Carolina); Plymouth Lighthouse (1769 in Massachusetts); Portsmouth Harbor Lighthouse (1771 in New Hampshire); and Cape Ann Lighthouse (1771 in Massachusetts).

Elevation or height of the focal plane

Fresnel lenses and most modern optical systems channel light signals into a narrow band known as the focal plane. Since the curvature of Earth would render low-lying lights practically worthless for navigation, a coastal beacon must have an elevated focal plane. The height of the plane above the water's surface—usually from 40 to 200 feet—helps determine the distance the light can travel.

Fixed signal

A lighthouse beacon that shines constantly during its regular hours of operation is said to display a "fixed" signal.

Flashing signal

A lighthouse beacon that turns on and off or grows much brighter at regular intervals is called a flashing signal.

Fog signal or foghorn

A distinct sound signal, usually a horn, trumpet, or siren, used to warn vessels away from prominent headlands or navigational obstacles during fog or other periods of low visibility.

Fresnel lenses

Invented in 1822 by Augustin Fresnel, a noted French physicist, Fresnel lenses concentrate light into a powerful beam that can be seen over great distances. Usually they consist of individual hand-polished glass prisms arrayed in a bronze frame. Manufactured by a number of French and British companies, these devices came in as

many as eleven different sizes or "orders." A massive first-order lens may be more than 6 feet in diameter and 12 feet tall, while a diminutive sixth-order lens is only about 1 foot wide and not much larger than an ordinary gallon jug.

Gallery

A circular walkway with a railing around the lantern of a lighthouse. Galleries provided keepers convenient access to the outside of the lantern for window cleaning, painting, and repair work.

Harbor light

A beacon intended to assist vessels moving in and out of a harbor. Not meant to serve as major coastal markers, harbor lights often consisted of little more than a lantern hung from a pole. However, many were official light stations with a tower and residence for the keeper. Some of these relatively modest beacons, such as the Derby Wharf Light in Salem, Massachusetts, remain in operation.

Investigation of 1851

Following a rash of shipwrecks during the late 1840s and the collapse of the Minots Ledge Lighthouse in 1851, Congress appointed a commission to investigate the nation's aids to navigation. Headed by Rear Admiral William B. Shubrick, the commission reported that the U.S. lighthouse system was at best shoddy and at worst a tragedy. In response Congress handed over authority of U.S. maritime aids to a nine-member Lighthouse Board, headed by Shubrick himself.

Keeper

Before the era of automation, responsibility for operating and maintaining a light station was placed in the hands of a keeper, sometimes aided by one or more assistants. During the eighteenth and nineteenth centuries, keepers were appointed by the Treasury Department or even the president himself in return for military service or a political favor. Although the work was hard and the pay minimal, these appointments were coveted since they offered a steady income and free housing.

Lamp and reflector

For several decades prior to the introduction of the highly efficient Fresnel lens, lighthouse beacons were intensified by means of lamp-and-reflector systems. These combined a bright-burning lamp and a polished mirror shaped in a manner intended to concentrate the light.

Lantern

The glass-enclosed space at the top of a light tower. It houses the lens (or optic) and protects it from the weather.

Lewis, Isaiah (I.W.P.)

A mid–nineteenth century civil engineer and lighthouse inspector, Lewis advocated construction of iron-skeleton light towers such as the failed Minots Ledge light tower off Cohasset, Massachusetts, and the more durable Carysfort Reef Lighthouse in the Florida Keys. Lewis was a vociferous critic of his uncle, the noted lighthouse contractor Winslow Lewis.

Lewis, Winslow

A former New England sea captain, Winslow Lewis built dozens of U.S. lighthouses during the first half of the nineteenth century. Lewis's bids for these projects were often quite low and the quality of the towers he built notoriously poor. Lewis introduced his own version of the Argand lamp and reflector system; many considered it vastly inferior to the original.

Light station

A navigational facility with a light beacon. Often the term is used interchangeably with "lighthouse," but a light station may not include a tower, quarters for a keeper, or a fog signal.

Light tower

A tall, often cylindrical, structure used to elevate a navigational light so that mariners can see it from a distance. Modern light towers support a lantern, which houses a lamp, electric beacon, or some other lighting device. Some light towers are an integral part of the keeper's residence, but most are detached.

Lighthouse Board

Beginning in 1851 and for more than half a century afterward, U.S. lighthouses were administered by nine-member Lighthouse Board. Usually board members were noted engineers, scientists, or military men. Creation of the board brought a fresh professional spirit and penchant for innovation to the Lighthouse Service. Perhaps the board's most significant contribution was its adoption of the advanced Fresnel lens as the standard U.S. lighthouse optic.

Lighthouse Service

A common term applied to the various organizations or agencies that built and maintained U.S. lighthouses from 1789 until 1939, when the Coast Guard was placed in charge.

Modern optic

A term referring to a broad array of lightweight, mostly weather-proof, devices that produce the most modern navigational lights.

Occulting or eclipsing light

There are several ways to produce a beacon that appears to flash. One is to "occult" or block the light at regular intervals, often with a rotating opaque panel.

Pleasonton, Stephen

A parsimonious Treasury Department auditor, Pleasonton took charge of the Lighthouse Service in 1820 and maintained a firm if not stifling grip on it for thirty years. Most historians agree that Pleasonton's tightfistedness encouraged low construction standards and delayed U.S. adoption of advanced optical technology for many years.

Private aid to navigation

A privately owned and maintained navigational light. Often, such lights are formerly deactivated beacons that have been reestablished for historic or aesthetic purposes.

Red sector

Some lighthouses display a multicolored beacon. For instance, an otherwise white beacon may appear red to mariners approaching a dangerous obstacle. Such navigational lights are said to have a "red sector."

Screw-pile towers

Open-water lighthouses built in rivers, bays, and other shallow water areas were often placed on piles that had been fitted with spiral flanges that made it possible to screw them into the subsurface sedimentary material. The screw piles often supported a lightweight wooden cottage with a small tower and lantern on its roof.

Skeleton towers

Iron- or steel-skeleton light towers consist of four or more heavily braced metal legs topped by workrooms and/or a lantern. Relatively durable and inexpensive, they were built in considerable numbers during the latter half of the nineteenth century. Since their open walls offer little resistance to wind and water, these towers proved ideal for offshore navigational stations, but some, such as the soaring skeleton tower at Marblehead near Salem, Massachusetts, were built on land.

Solar-powered optic

Nowadays many remote lighthouse beacons are powered by batteries recharged during the day by solar panels.

Sparkplug, teakettle, or coffeepot lights

Many open-water lighthouses in northern climates are built on round, concrete-filled caissons that protect them from fast-flowing water and ice floes. Usually the massive caissons are black while the cylindrical iron towers on top of them are painted white, giving them the appearance of an automobile sparkplug. However, some think they look more like teakettles or coffeepots.

Twin light

A few lighthouses, such as those at Cape Ann or Chatham in Massachusetts, once exhibited two separate lights. This was done to distinguish the beacon from other prominent nearby lights.

Worthylake, George

Generally recognized by historians as America's first lighthouse keeper, George Worthylake accepted a job tending Boston Light on Little Brewster Island in 1716. The following year Worthylake's career as a keeper ended tragically when he drowned in a boating accident.

ABOUT THE AUTHORS

Photographs by **Bruce Roberts** have appeared in numerous magazines, including *Life* and *Sports Illustrated*, and in hundreds of books, many of them about lighthouses. He was director of photography at *Southern Living* magazine for many years. His work is also on display in the permanent collection at the Smithsonian Institution. He lives in Morehead City, North Carolina.

Ray Jones is the author or coauthor of fourteen best-selling books about lighthouses. He has served as an editor at Time-Life Books, as founding editor of *Albuquerque Living* magazine, as writing coach at *Southern Living* magazine, and as founding publisher of Country Roads Press. He lives in Pebble Beach, California, where he continues to write about lighthouses and serves as a consultant to businesses, publishers, and other authors.